EDUCATION AND THE NATURE OF KNOWLEDGE

NEW PATTERNS OF LEARNING SERIES
Edited by P.J. Hills, University of Leicester

AN INTRODUCTION TO EDUCATIONAL COMPUTING
Nicholas John Rushby

PREPARING EDUCATIONAL MATERIALS
N.D.C. Harris

THE ORGANISATION AND MANAGEMENT OF
EDUCATIONAL TECHNOLOGY
Richard N. Tucker

ADULT LEARNING
R. Bernard Lovell

EVALUATING INSTRUCTIONAL TECHNOLOGY
Christopher Kay Knapper

ASSESSING STUDENTS, APPRAISING TEACHING
John C. Clift and Bradford W. Imrie

STUDENT LEARNING IN HIGHER EDUCATION
John D. Wilson

LEARNING AND VISUAL COMMUNICATION
David Sless

RESOURCE-BASED LEARNING FOR HIGHER AND
CONTINUING EDUCATION
John Clarke

LEARNING TO LEARN IN HIGHER EDUCATION
Jean Wright

PROFESSIONAL EDUCATION
P. Jarvis

Education and the Nature of Knowledge

R.J. Brownhill

CROOM HELM
London & Canberra

© 1983 R.J. Brownhill
Croom Helm Ltd, Provident House, Burrell Row, Beckenham, Kent BR3 1AT

British Library Cataloguing in Publication Data

Brownhill, R.J.
　Education and the nature of knowledge. —
　(New patterns of learning series)
　1. Education psychology
　2. Education — Aims and objectives
　I. Title　II. Series
　370.15′2　　LB1051

ISBN 0-7099-0654-4

Printed and bound in Great Britain by
Biddles Ltd, Guildford and King's Lynn

CONTENTS

Introduction		vii
1.	The Nature of Knowledge	9
2.	The Organisation of Experience	23
3.	Tacit Knowledge	37
4.	Teaching and Learning	51
5.	The Social Context of Knowledge	65
6.	The Scientific Community: Actuality and Morality	77
7.	Education, Control and the Judicial Community	87
8.	An Intellectual and a Non-intellectual Community: History and Morality	99
9.	Argument and Persuasion	110
10.	Conclusion: Objectivity and Education	121
Index		133

INTRODUCTION

One of the most important functions of a teacher is to pass on a certain body of knowledge to his pupils. Yet at the same time it is expected that he will also pass on techniques of reasoning, which can be associated with this knowledge, in order that the pupils will develop the ability to make discoveries, come to conclusions, and criticise and estimate the usefulness and rationality of this knowledge themselves.

It is important, then, to understand what is meant by knowledge and what is meant by 'techniques of reasoning'. The paradigm form of knowledge has been taken to be that expressed by the scientist. However, a considerable literature has developed criticising the nature of the scientist's claim. Paul Feyerabend goes so far as to claim that there is no method of science and that scientific decision making is akin to aesthetic appreciation. Much of this criticism has arisen from a historical and sociological analysis of the activity of scientists but Michael Polanyi bases his criticism on an analysis of the nature of knowledge and on a reappraisal of the concept of objectivity. His major innovation is an analysis of the very process of discovery, and his introduction of the concept of tacit knowledge. Explicit knowledge exists within a framework of tacit concepts which are rarely expressed and are partly unexpressible. Knowledge can only be understood within the framework of this context. Discovery, then, is a matter of skill and judgment within a particular framework and can only be understood and estimated by people who work within similar frameworks. Education consists of inculcating pupils into these frameworks. It gives the pupils a way of looking at things but it also gives them the values and techniques of these frameworks and the ability to criticise within them and make judgments. Michael Oakeshott argues that education is the initiation of a pupil into a tradition. Into the skills and practices of his own community. Knowledge is essentially a practical skill, a judgment, a knowing how.

Both Polanyi and Oakeshott, although saying something which is very important about the nature of general education, are also saying something of especial importance about the nature of professional education; what it is and what it entails. This book then puts special emphasis on the developments of skills and judgments (thereby going some way to deny the 'knowing how' and the 'knowing that' distinction), it examines the structure of intellectual and professional communities, and explores in detail the nature of professional education.

1 THE NATURE OF KNOWLEDGE

In teaching children one of the functions a teacher has is to pass on to his pupils a body of knowledge, whether that is a knowledge in a specialised field such as physics, history or maths or more generalised fields. With younger children in particular, we would expect that certain moral notions should be passed on and with very young children some attempt would be made to correct their manners.

This seems a common enough statement but nowadays it would be controversial and only partially acceptable. In these specialised subjects most people would still talk about passing on a body of knowledge. They would agree that there is something definite to teach but they would be suspicious of the idea that we should pass on moral knowledge. Is it, for instance, possible to do such a thing, for does a body of moral knowledge exist? Is not morality related somehow to our feelings, perhaps our prejudices? In other words is not morality subjective, my morality and not yours or at most intersubjective, our morality not theirs? Leon Trotsky even wrote a book entitled *Their Morals and Ours*, which indicated that terms like goodness and justice related merely to the interests of a class, and had no universal application. How can we then possibly give morality the status of knowledge and even talk sensibly about moral education? We should rather be talking about our own moral prejudices, and the inculcation of these prejudices into unsuspecting pupils.

Not so long ago such an analysis of morality would have been considered anarchistic or at most an expression of an extreme left-wing view aimed at destroying the very structure of society. Nowadays it is quite acceptable and commonplace. Students often, when making a moral statement, say that it is 'Just my opinion, it need not be yours' or 'People can believe what they like' and 'We shouldn't force our views on others'. No universal claim is made for their opinion. They are not claiming that it is a piece of knowledge which they hold and which can be checked by others, and then followed by others. They are then, in effect, denying morality the status of knowledge.

It can be argued that this now prevalent attitude reflects not only the political views of the Marxists but the revolution in ethical theory which took place earlier this century, and which has now seeped down from the intellectual sphere to the ordinary man. The work of writers such as A.J. Ayer and C.L. Stevenson[1] come to mind generally pigeon-holed under the title of the emotivist theory of ethics. It is also true that many ethical theorists have moved from this position so now there is a spate of books on practical ethics, even animal rights, and, of course, moral education. But behind them remains the nagging fear that perhaps the emotivists are right, and that our moral opinions are subjective and relative.

However, this subjectivism and relativism is not only confined to the moral sphere — it has more recently turned its lance at the paradigm example of a body of knowledge: science.

Yet if there is not a body of scientific knowledge, if science is merely intersubjective opinion where scientists put forward their prejudices as if they were the truth then this must have a profound effect on our status as educators. Are we merely pushing into our children opinions which are by no means certain, arbitrary beliefs whose only claim to the truth is that a group of self-styled specialists indicate that they like them? Of course it can be argued that such an argument is silly for it is only a group of cranky philosophers and revolutionary sociologists who believe (presumably not know as they would then be allowing the possibility of objectivity) such things, and it need not concern the educator, who can continue to teach as if he were revealing chunks of knowledge to children. But then how could we distinguish ourselves from the indoctrinator, as we would be teaching as pieces of knowledge, opinions, which we knew were doubtful, as if they were the truth? We could, of course, teach our children to use their critical faculties, and to suspect what was taught them. But this in itself would be a peculiar way of teaching as it would tend to reduce children's confidence in their teacher, and wonder about the whole process of education. In any case how can a person just be critical; criticism cannot just arise in a vacuum, it must arise from certain points of view? It also assumes that there is some point in criticism, where there is no point in criticising prejudices as it will have no effect on them. In any case neither the pupil nor probably the teacher would have a sufficient degree of expertise in the language game of the specialist to question, on their own terms, their beliefs. And even if they could, if subjectivism is accepted, it would have no significance outside the game.

An understanding and acceptance of the subjectivist position could well bring the educational idea of passing on bodies of knowledge to a grinding halt. Why bother to pass on prejudices to others particularly when they are not our own prejudices but those of a suspect elite. The point of education would have vanished, at least for the teacher with integrity. (Notice how destructive the subjectivist argument is for under it no one could really act with integrity but only do things they liked.)

I propose then to look briefly at this revolution in the theory of knowledge in order to see the type of problem it raises for the educator.

Objective Knowledge

When we talk about knowledge being objective we are making certain assumptions about what it must mean to say something is objective. We are really referring to certain criteria of objectivity and these criteria are themselves open to argument and debate. They need to be established by argument and to that extent are optional alternatives, and different writers may have different criteria. The criteria I refer to then may differ from other authors' and are open to challenge but a thoroughgoing objectivist must argue that in principle we must be able to agree on the criteria, and that in principle there cannot be optional alternatives but only one set of criteria. I will list five features a piece of knowledge must have if it is to be accepted as objective:

1. The knowledge must refer to a reality which is separate from ourselves, and this entails that a distinction has to be drawn between what the world is and what we happen to say about it. All of us could believe a certain thing about reality but we could all be mistaken, as our beliefs cannot change reality. Likewise it is possible for a certain person to have a belief about reality which is in conflict with all other people's beliefs but if his belief coincides with what reality is then his belief is correct.

2. As there is an independent reality we can test our beliefs by reference to this reality and without this possibility of testability

there can be no objectivity. For instance, Sir Karl Popper[2] would argue that for a theory to be classed as a scientific theory it must be put in a testable form. The idea here is that nature itself is a judge of a belief's validity.

3. In referring to the objectivity of science we are talking about the ideas of science as being objective. We are concerned with theories about facts, theories about the relationship of one set of facts to another, theories about the relationship of our beliefs to other beliefs and their relationship to the original facts. We test theories rather than for the existence of the original facts themselves. We are concerned with such things as measurement, relationship and prediction. Michael Polanyi[3] brings out this point when he argues that scientists considered the Copernican theory to be more objective than Ptolemaic cosmology as they attributed greater objectivity to theoretical knowledge than that gained through the senses. Theoretical knowledge is not tied to our senses but must stand on its own feet.

4. A theory must be able to stand on its own feet like a map with its own independent status and rationality. The objective status of a theory has nothing to do with our commitment to it, as our own personal tastes are irrelevant to its truth. For instance, a person who gets lost when he correctly follows a map will attribute the mistake to the map and not to himself. The point being that in the case of a scientific theory it is not the person putting forward the theory who is proved wrong when the theory fails but the theory. In order to achieve this status of independence a theory must have an explicitness as a system of rules, which is separate from sense experience. Ideally it should be in a mathematical form which can be understood by and demand acceptance from other rational beings.

5. This brings out another aspect of an objective theory. It has to have public communicability so that we can understand it whatever our location or situation. It should not depend on our own situation but be an independent form of public knowledge. Polanyi again indicates this when he points out that the Ptolemaic system depended for its rationality on our earthbound situation but the Copernican system commended itself to dwellers on any planet.

The objective status of a scientific theory then lies in the fact that it is impersonal, with an independent status of its own, which claims universal recognition, and that it can be checked by reference to a separate reality. This is also the Popperian notion of the autonomy of ideas. When they are created they become independent of their creator and stand or fall on their own ability to reveal reality.

Certainty and Doubt

There are numerous difficulties with these 'criteria of objectivity'. It is all very well stating that there is a world separate to our beliefs but how do we know what this reality is as we have only our own beliefs. Do we rely on some other authority or on our own authority, or do we deny the reality of all things or claim that things are really the creation of our own mind?

Descartes provides the prime example of a philosopher who was searching for certainty, and in doing so produced an excessively individualistic approach to the understanding of reality. Knowledge and certainty could be gained by the individual knower who was prepared to follow the Cartesian method of constructive scepticism. This entailed doubting all our previous beliefs until we arrived at some point where we could doubt no longer. Thus Descartes' famous *cogito, ergo sum* — I think therefore I am. We could arrive at certain clear and distinct ideas which we knew were sound and could not be doubted. The clear and distinct ideas could be classed as self evident, and on their foundation we could re-build a more certain world in the way a geometrician developed his propositions. Mathematics was to be taken as the model for the acquisition of knowledge but in practice, as Descartes himself was to find, this was to prove difficult, as the real world cannot always be explained with mathematical precision. Nevertheless he still believed that certainty in principle was possible.

The Cartesian method is in fact a way of sorting out things before one's mind so that they are accessible to one's understanding. When one has put it in the right order one is able to see it completely, to understand its reasonableness and able to prevent oneself lapsing into error. The individual knower through his attentive mind is able to grasp and know that which is true.

As can be seen the Cartesian method is itself an attack on any reliance on the authority of others, although Deseartes carefully develops his argument so as to avoid the censure of the Universal Church. He argued on what grounds can authority be claimed? Can it be claimed on the basis of the status of the so-called authority or on the institutional base of the claimant? This is extremely doubtful for in practice we find that authorities in all subjects are continually disputing and arguing. No, it can only be claimed by the individual knower, who through the pure light of reason has arrived at clear and distinct ideas.

However, behind this confidence in the power of the attentive mind, and of the individual knower to move from infallible intuition to infallible intuition along his path of certainty, lay a nagging doubt. A doubt which was frightening and unacceptably so for Descartes, for how could we know that these clear and distinct ideas actually gave us infallible knowledge. Descartes writes:

> And indeed, as I have no reason to believe that there is a deceitful God, or as, moreover, I have not yet considered the reasons which prove there is a God at all, the reason for doubting which depends on a supposition is very slight, and, so to speak, metaphysical. But in order to be able to remove this doubt completely I must inquire whether there is a God, as soon as the opportunity presents itself; and if I find there is one, I must also inquire whether he can be deceitful; for without the knowledge of these two truths, I do not see that I can be certain of anything.[4]

The certainty of the clear and distinct ideas then depends on the existence of God, and the existence of a non-deceitful God at that, but then how could the Christian God be deceitful when he had all the perfections?

The Cartesian ideas became all conquering; science developed with confidence and through the initiatives of great men. But a hundred years after the publication of Descartes' *Discourse on Method*, with the publication of David Hume's *Treatise on Human Nature* in 1739-40 came a time bomb which challenged the whole concept of scientific certainty, and which through its influence has dominated thinking about the philosophy of science and ethics this century.

Hume develops his attack on the idea of certainty by asking what is the basis of scientific reasoning, and comes to the conclusion that our reasoning about the world has to be based on the relation of cause and effect. Our attempt in the physical sciences is to find out why there are regularities in nature, and then attempt to produce such an explanation by revealing the causes of such regularities. If we could find out the true causes of such regularities then we had certainty in science, and succeeded in achieving the aim of the Cartesian method.

Hume points out that it is only because we believe in the existence of fixed and immutable causal connections that we develop the confidence to make predictions about future happenings. We believe that if we start a fire under a kettle of water and keep that fire going then the water will eventually boil. We believe that if we push a person's head under water and hold him down long enough he will drown. We have implicit faith that these are regularities in nature and that these regularities will remain constant. Indeed if we did not believe this then there would be no point in carrying out research, as we would have no belief that the results of our research would remain constant, or that experiments could even be repeated, or even, for that matter, that night would follow day.

Yet what is the basis for our belief, for have we a guarantee that the future will be like the past, and if we have then what is this guarantee? Medieval philosophers had talked about necessity; that things had to happen in a certain way because of their very nature, for being what they were. They believed that there were eternal immutable substances in nature and these substances had within themselves certain hidden powers that guaranteed that they always behaved in the same way. Such an argument creates an obvious problem. If these powers are hidden how do we know they are there, and even if we believe that these powers caused certain happenings in the past how do we know that they will in the future?

This is really stating the problem of induction, and Hume points out that there is no adequate reason to suppose that what has happened in the past will repeat itself in situations not examined. Our belief, for instance, that A causes B is not based on any necessary connection between A and B but is based on our experience that in fact B does follow A. He states that our knowledge of causal relations 'arises entirely from the uniformity observable in the operations of nature, where similar objects are constantly conjoined together, and the mind is determined by custom to infer the one from the appearance of the other'.[5] Our knowledge then is based on a belief not a necessary connection.

Yet if the validity of injunction is challenged in this way then only two approaches seem open to us. We can either develop a 'philosophy of belief' or steer clear of mere belief and try to rely in some way on deduction.

Popper puts it succinctly when referring to the effect the destruction of induction had on Hume:

> By these results Hume himself — one of the most rational minds ever — was turned into a sceptic and, at the same time a believer in an irrationalist epistemology. His result that repetition has no power whatever as an argument, although it dominates our cognitive life or our 'understanding', led him to the conclusion that argument or reason plays only a minor role in our understanding. Our knowledge is earmarked as being not only in the nature of a belief, but of a rationally indefensible belief — of an irrational faith.[6]

Nevertheless a philosophy of belief is in fact a possible alternative for Hume but he made a manoeuvre which, if accepted, would limit any potential it had for explaining the nature of science. He does this by disallowing the possibility of generalising beliefs and states, 'We can never be induced to believe any matter of fact, except where its cause, or its effect is present.'[7] and that causation is the only relation which 'can be traced beyond our senses and informs us of existences and objects we do not see and feel.'[8] H.H. Price suggests that Hume would probably also accept an addition to this: 'constant conjunctions in which the conjuncta are co-existent, not successive — regularities of concomitance, as opposed to regularities of sequence.'[9] Beliefs arising from constant conjunctions then are reasonable, as they come directly from our experience but if they do not arise from this sort of experience they must be unreasonable. A reasonable person is one who learns from experience, and behaves accordingly and the reasonableness in this case is an inductive reasonableness not a deductive one.

As Price points out the doctrine of belief which Hume develops is a very narrow one and does not allow the development of generalisations — for instance, water expands when it freezes. It therefore cannot be used as a basis for developing science. Price states: 'It will not apply to general beliefs about matters of fact but only beliefs about particular matters of fact. This is because he insists that an idea which we believe must be related to or associated with a present impression.'[10]

Karl Popper while accepting Hume's criticism of induction rejects any attempt to move towards a philosophy of belief which he argues must be irrational, subjective and doomed to failure. His attempt is to maintain science as an objective pursuit while recognising that we cannot use induction to undertake this task. He proposes then a hypothetico-deductive framework which makes use of the logical truism that a universal proposition can be conclusively falsified by one counter example, and in doing so also rejects the notion that unrestricted universal propositions can be verified by finite exemplifications. For example, we cannot prove all swans are white by producing 5 million white swans but we can show they are not by producing one black one. Popper points out that there is a difference between the logic of his argument and his methodology. In logic we can disprove a universal proposition by one counter example, in practice in the scientific community, and dealing with scientific hypotheses we would need to build up a number of falsifying instances until it became generally acceptable that the hypotheses were false.

Popper's interest then is in developing an objective science and he believes that science consists of a tentative body of ideas which are continually tested against reality. His aim is to formulate daring hypotheses which lead to the continual growth of science. In order to achieve this he suggests that scientific statements should be put in a form that will allow them to be falsified — they should be negative existential statements. Statements put in this form can be classed as scientific statements but statements we cannot falsify, like an existential statement, we can class as metaphysical.[11] He believes that in fact science grows by the continual criticism of hypotheses which when falsified are then replaced by new hypotheses which explain the falsifying instance, and lead to new discoveries but are themselves open to refutation. He therefore deplores attempts to protect hypotheses from falsification tests by, for instance, the development of further ad hoc hypotheses whose sole function is to save the original hypotheses. A good hypothesis should have a high information content with a probability approaching zero but should nevertheless be able to stand up to criticism. For example, a statement that it would rain in England some day in April which was correct would be of little interest but a statement that it would rain in a certain part of the Sahara desert on the 22nd April at 15.00 hours and was correct would be of great interest. It would have a high information content with a low probability and have stood up to a test.

There are a number of features in Popper's theory which are of interest for our purpose. He is claiming that a hypothesis must stand on its own feet and it is therefore irrelevant who makes it or to what extent the person making it is committed to it. The hypothesis must be put forward in a way which will allow it to be tested against reality. In other words, we can say that the hypothesis makes an impersonal claim and is tested against an independent reality. It is also public in the sense that both the hypothesis and the test are accessible to anyone (who has the ability and interest to understand) not just to the cognoscente.

The Popperian proposals then are both realist and objectivist and for a time began to dominate the philosophy of science. But notice it is still related to the Cartesian desire for certainty. The truth is no longer manifest and science is tentative and will remain tentative for ever, but at least we can get rid of false scientific hypotheses, and we can distinguish scientific statements from metaphysical ones by putting scientific statements in a testable form. We can at least know that we are mistaken.

Relativism and Subjectivism

The main criticism of the Popperian notion of science has arisen from a sociological/historical viewpoint exemplified by T.S. Kuhn in his *Structure of Scientific Revolutions*.[12] His position denies any objective stance. Kuhn makes a distinction between normal science and revolutionary science. The practice of normal science takes place within certain paradigms, accepted current theories to which scientists are committed. He argues that scientists rarely challenge these paradigms by bold conjectures and tests but accept them, and merely solve certain puzzles within them. The paradigms, in a sense, form the rules of the game which defines the puzzle the scientist attempts to solve. Indeed, without a paradigm, Kuhn argues, a scientist would not be able to distinguish the important from the trivial and irrelevant. The paradigm then gives to the scientist a conceptual tool which enables him to view the world in a certain way. Yet if a scientist fails to solve a puzzle within current theory he does not then divert his appraisal on to current theory itself but assumes that it is his own expertise that is at fault: that he has not made a proper use of the hypotheses available within the paradigm. Peculiarly, then, in normal science it is not current theory which is tested but the ability of the puzzle solver.

Kuhn argues that Popper is mainly concerned with the growth of science, and believes that science does in fact grow by a revolutionary overthrow of an accepted theory and not by puzzle solving, which brings about the gradual accretion of knowledge. In order to achieve this the Popperian tests are designed to put current theory under maximum strain but Kuhn argues that instances of this actually happening are very rare. They only happen when a crisis already exists, or a theory exists which is competing with present approaches to research (for example, Einstein's general relativity theory in the early part of this century). These revolutionary periods bring about what Kuhn calls 'extraordinary research', and certainly do then exhibit the characteristics Popper wants. However, these rare occurences cannot be used to describe the whole scientific enterprise. It is in these revolutionary periods that a scientist acts more like a philosopher than a scientist, for a philosopher is concerned with continual criticism of basic concepts and a scientist is not. A scientist's task is gradually to increase knowledge while relying on accepted theory, and importantly his whole training is to do this.

Kuhn tells us that a scientist cannot easily switch from one paradigm to another for they are 'incommensurable'. He means by this that their content cannot be compared, so that what is important in one theory may be unimportant in another, or may not even exist in that theory. Furthermore the vocabulary used in incommensurable theories may have different meanings so that we are therefore unable even to understand different theories by reference to some neutral language. In fact under attack he admits the languages may be translatable but the translations will not be able to get all the nuances and hidden meanings of the language, which are only available to a person who is committed to and works within a language.

The switch from one paradigm to another cannot be a gradual process brought about by the failure of a paradigm one is within, and the recognition of the good features in another, but is a sort of gestalt switch, a sudden conversion which replaces a commitment to one paradigm by a firm commitment to another.

Science, then, for Kuhn is more akin to our idea of a religion. We have to have faith in a paradigm if we are to use it for puzzle solving, and we have to be adept at the rules of the game. We must learn and understand the mysterious language of the paradigm, which is virtually inaccessible to people outside our game. The paradigm provides our conceptual apparatus, 'That is why a law which cannot even be demonstrated to one group of scientists may occasionally seem intuitively obvious to another'.[13] We are committed first and then our reasons, or rather rationalisations, for the commitment follow. Furthermore we do not check our findings against an independent reality, and we cannot do so as this would suggest that methods of approach exist, and a neutral language exists, which is separate to our paradigms. In other words, if two scientists are arguing from within different paradigms then we cannot say that one is right and that the other is wrong, but only that their paradigms are in conflict, and that one will eventually be accepted and the other rejected. And that if then the scientist whose theory is rejected goes on supporting it then he will be considered an out-of-date crank and no longer a scientist.

Paul Feyerabend[14] takes even further this subjectivist and relativist approach to science. He argues that preference for one scientific theory over another is merely a matter of aesthetic appreciation; a matter of taste.

As can be expected the destruction of the objectivity of the major example of a body of knowledge, science, can be found to apply to other spheres as well. Wittgenstein has argued that the testing of hypotheses must take place within a system, 'The system is not so much the point of departure, as the elements in which arguments have their life.'[15] The point he is making is that we can only argue from within our own view of the world, and the arguments we use may well not be acceptable or even understandable to a person with another view. Reasons that seem good to us are only good reasons within particular commitments, and if we have different viewpoints then we can only resort to persuasion and rhetoric.

Yet, if as Kuhn and Wittgenstein indicate, notions of right and wrong, truth and falsehood, apply only within certain paradigms, language games or systems, and cannot be used outside them, then what of any concept of an independent reality? Can reality have an existence separate to a particular game? I think, in a way, it is not being denied that a separate reality exists, and it is not being argued that we create reality. What is being argued is that as far as we are concerned it is irrelevant whether it exists or not. We create our concepts, and they are judged and tested in our own terms. Actual reality has nothing to do with it. Peter Winch argues:

> Reality is not what gives language sense. What is real and what is unreal shows itself in the sense that language has. Further both the distinction between the real and the unreal and the concept of agreement with reality themselves belong to our language.[16]

Interestingly it is possible to hold that there is an independent reality, while still arguing that 'reality' cannot be looked at independently of our own conceptual schemata, and that it is possible that people looking at the world with different schemata may be looking at it in a completely different way to ourselves. Nevertheless it does not seem to be an entirely coherent viewpoint.

Conclusion

Recent writings in the sociology and history of science and in philosophy have suggested that we cannot talk of objective bodies of knowledge but only of subjective beliefs or at best intersubjective beliefs. This raises a number of questions for the educator. For instance, should we think of education as the method of inculcating into pupils particular views of the world, of giving them certain cultural spectacles? If we should, then does this in its turn mean that specialised education and even education for the professions can only develop within this general situation; a paradigm within a paradigm?

The argument also entails that we as educators also look at the process of education from within certain paradigms, and that we cannot get outside and examine them with neutral language and objective assessment. This raises the most important question of all: Is it possible, while accepting the general approach of the

Wittgenstein/Kuhn argument to establish the objectivity of the knowledge gained, and the non-arbitrariness of processes of education?

Notes

1. C.f. A.J. Ayer, *Language, Truth and Logic* (Victor Gollancz, London, 1936). C.L. Stevenson, *Ethics and Language* (Yale University Press, London, 1945).
2. K.R. Popper, *The Logic of Scientific Discovery* (Hutchinson, London, 1959).
3. M. Polanyi, *Personal Knowledge* (Routledge, London, 1958), p. 4.
4. R. Descartes, *Discourse on Method and the Meditations* (Penguin, Harmondsworth, Third Meditation, 1968), p. 115.
5. D. Hume, *An Inquiry Concerning Human Understanding* (Hendel Edn, New York, 1959), p. 92.
6. K.R. Popper, *Objective Knowledge* (Oxford University Press, Oxford, 1972), pp. 4-5.
7. D. Hume, *Treatise on Human Nature* (Selby Bigge Edn, Oxford, 1906), p. 623.
8. Ibid.
9. H.H. Price, *Belief*, London (1969), p. 176.
10. Ibid p. 180.
11. Popper calls this the problem of demarcation. 'My solution is the principle that a statement is empirical if these are (finite) conjunctions of singular empirical statements ("basic statements" or "test statements") which contradict it. It is a consequence of this that an isolated purely existential statement (such as "there exists a sea serpent somewhere in the world at some time") is not an empirical statement.' Popper, *Objective Knowledge*, p. 12.
12. T.S. Kuhn, *The Structure of Scientific Revolutions* (Chicago University Press, Chicago, Illinois, 1962).
13. Ibid. p. 144.
14. P. Feyerabend, *Against Method* (NLB, London, 1975).
15. L. Wittgenstein, *On Certainty* (Oxford University Press, Oxford, 1969), sect. 105.
16. P. Winch, Understanding a Primitive Society', in D.Z. Phillips (ed.), *Religion and Understanding* (Oxford University Press, Oxford, 1967), p. 13.

2 THE ORGANISATION OF EXPERIENCE

In this chapter I want to examine in more detail the concept of a system of ideas. Of especial interest for our purpose are the theories about our organisation of experience developed by the social philosopher Michael Oakeshott in the 1930s, and in particular his concept of 'modes of experience'. Not only do these theories foreshadow the present debate on the nature of knowledge but form the base for the later development of Oakeshott's political philosophy and philosophy of education with its particular emphasis on the development of judgment and learning of skills. I also propose to briefly examine the complementary concept of the interpretative framework developed by the philosopher of science, Michael Polanyi. He argues that all judgments must take place within certain interpretative frameworks, and that the sort of judgments we make in our intellectual activity are prefigured by the sort of judgments animals make in their everyday life.

Points of View and Modes of Experience

It is commonly argued when dispute arises and incompatible positions emerge that the dispute must be based on a disagreement about what the facts are. It is further argued that if the dispute cannot be traced back to a disagreement of this sort then the dispute can only be classed as irrational, and based merely on the prejudice of the participants. For example, if we have a dispute between A and B and factual agreement, which we can call $a \ldots n$, and A then tries to persuade B that the action he proposes is justified by reference to f, g and h, we have the problem that B has already agreed on f, g and h and has therefore taken them into account when deciding on his own opinion. As this is the case he cannot be persuaded to change his opinion by reference to these facts. Is it possible then for him to be persuaded to change his opinion? Of course he can but the argument entails that he cannot change it on rational grounds, the dispute can only be irrational and has to be settled either by one or the other shouting the other down, by force or by some other persuasive technique. You cannot through rational argument get agreement but one side can acquiesce or the dispute can continue.

This argument does not seem satisfactory. It is certainly the case that we can sometimes get people to agree by indicating that certain facts have not been taken into account but it does not follow that if all the facts have been taken into account then the dispute must be irrational. For example, in looking at a piece of literature we can have a dispute about the significance of a particular part of a novel or a play, or in looking at a philosopher's argument we may have a dispute about the nature of the argument he is putting forward. In both cases there may be no dispute about the text itself — the facts — but how to interpret the text. We may also claim that a particular interpretation is an especially good interpretation or even better than another one because it gives a greater insight into the meaning of the text. It may give a meaning to a previously obscure passage and by doing this fit the work together more adequately as a whole. In an extreme case it may even lead us to look at the work in a completely new light.

The notion of looking at things in a new light applies much more widely. In the example given disputes can arise about whether one interpretation is better than another, whether it gives a greater insight into the author's meaning but nevertheless, although these disputes cannot be resolved by reference to the neutral facts themselves, the text, they do remain within the attempt to understand the meaning of the text. We can, however, take the same facts and look at them in an entirely different way. Michael Polanyi gives an interesting example of this. For instance we may look at facts and relate them to a task we wish to achieve. He gives the example of a wish we may have to hang something on a wall. In order to achieve this wish we will need to have a concept of a hammer and have some notion of what hammers are like or what objects are potential hammers. He states, 'The suitability of an object to serve as a hammer is an observable property, but it can be observed only within the framework defined by the performance it is supposed to serve.'[2]

The point he is making is that objects are classed as hammers only when we look at them in that context: a heel of a shoe will only be looked at as a hammer when we desire to hammer something into something else — when we look at it under the general framework of a useful performance with the specific task of hammering the nail into the wall. Notice also that this example is teleological as we are aiming at a useful performance. We move from the view of an object with an observable property to a practical knowledge that the object is useful for hammering the nail into the wall. However, examples can be given which are not of this type, for instance, in the case of a doctor making a diagnosis. He will not be concerned with every fact about the object, his patient, but will look for facts which can be classed as symptoms. He will then attempt to fit these symptoms into a pattern so that he can diagnose the illness. We could argue that this is still teleological as the diagnosis is aiming at future treatment. This is so but taken by itself it is not teleological as we could after all consider the diagnosis either correct or incorrect whether or not we went on to the next stage of the diagnosis.

These different examples of the interpretation of texts, the use of observable objects for practical purposes, and the doctor's diagnosis indicate that disputes can be rational even when there is no dispute about the actual facts themselves. The disputes are about whether a particular interpretation gives a better interpretation of the facts, whether a particular object is useful for a practical activity, and whether a particular pattern of symptoms can form the basis of a correct diagnosis.[3]

The hammer example and the diagnosis example also make it clear that we can look at the same objects from entirely different points of view. For instance, we can look at a beautiful little stone dog from a utilitarian point of view, 'Will it bang this nail into the wall?' or from an aesthetic point of view, 'What a charming piece of sculpture'. We can look at a body from a diagnostic point of view or perhaps an artistic one. Certain features of objects are given their significance by the particular context we look at them in, and under a different context the very same facts may have little significance or no significance. In other words we look at things from different points of view and therefore different features of them become important. John Brennan makes this point when he states, 'Any features of an object are significant only within a given context meaning.'[4]

Clearly in our everyday life we continually look at things from different points of view. The question arises as to how we make the sort of judgments we do make when we make decisions within points of view. Decisions are really judgments about how we are going to do something or what we are going to say about something. For example, say I state that a particular theft was a clever robbery. I am looking at the robbery from a technical point of view. How difficult was it to plan? How complicated was it, what obstacles were overcome, how efficiently was it carried out? Taking these factors into consideration I make the judgment that it was a clever robbery. I could, of course, look at it from the moral point of view and in that case the technical expertise exhibited in concluding the robbery would be irrelevant. I would be concerned with the fact that a person's property was stolen; I will wonder whether violence was used. What I would be doing in looking at the robbery would be making an appraisal by referring to different standards, and under different points of view, differing standards would be relevant. From the technical point of view standards of efficiency and technical expertise would be relevant, and from the moral point of view standards of conduct relevant. Furthermore it would be only by referring to these standards that certain features of the case, the facts, would become important.

When we make judgments about things we look at them from distinct points of view, and make reference to the standards appropriate to that point of view and it is this that makes certain facts relevant and certain facts not, and which gives meaning to the neutral facts.

This type of argument can be developed even further for not only do we look at things from different points of view, and give things meaning by the way we look at them, but we organise our whole experience under different points of view or forms of thought. Michael Oakeshott, developing such an argument, calls these forms of thought 'modes of experience'.

Oakeshott points out that we tend to divide experience for analytical purposes into 'experiencing' and 'what is experienced' but that in fact these can only be abstract concepts, as in practice there can be no way of dividing them. They do not determine each other but stand to each other in interdependence, 'they compose a single whole.'[5] Nevertheless it is true that for analytical purposes we can make certain distinctions within the concept of experience, for instance, thought, mere consciousness, sensation, perception, intuition and so forth but the distinctions are not absolute, 'experience everywhere, not merely is inseparable from thought, but is itself a form of thought.'[6] The abstract concepts like perception and intuition are 'lifeless abstractions' and ask to be joined to the concrete whole from which they come:

> All abstract and incomplete experience is a modification of what is complete, individual and concrete, and to this it must be referred if we are to ascertain its character. And thought or judgment, as I see it, is not one form of experience, but is itself the concrete whole of experience.[7]

Oakeshott's argument here is that the distinctions we can make are abstractions which have no real meaning unless they are related to the concrete whole which in fact gives them their meaning. He also denies that things like sensation or perception are separate forms of experience in themselves.

The usual attempt to distinguish them lies in the argument that immediate perceptions and sensations do not involve judgment; we see a green blob and only then do we judge it to be a green leaf, we feel a sensation and only then do we judge it to be a certain type of sensation. Oakeshott's not altogether convincing reply is that although it is difficult to deny this difference he is unable to conclude that this actual sensation and perception do not involve a judgment. It may be possible to separate sensation and perception from certain specific judgments but not possible to separate them from all judgments, for instance, presumably in this case the judgment that the green blob is a green blob and then the further judgment that it is a leaf. He states: 'We perceive only that which we in some sense recognise, that which has some meaning or significance for us; and where there is a meaning or significance there is judgment.'[8]

He denies then that there is any part of experience which is less than judgment but also denies that there can be a form of experience which is more than judgment: that there can be some part of experience which transcends thought. For instance, it is sometimes argued that intuition can give us an immediate insight into the nature of reality. This claim could be examined either in a psychological sense or a logical sense. The psychological sense sometimes postulates a sudden flash of the mind over and above the process of thought which gives you an answer to a problem. However the notion of giving an answer involves a judgment. The mind must be already oriented onto the object to be examined before insights can be achieved; one has to have a notion as to what the problem is before one can solve it. Intuition in this sense can only be a speeding up of the thought process not a matter of no thought and no judgment.

Intuition in the logical sense is more complicated and suggests a notion of direct understanding, a direct subject-predicate experience, which goes beyond judgment. One does not judge an intuition to be true — one knows that it is true. This concept of intuition then suggests that there is a form of understanding which is more direct, immediate and certain than the process of judgment with its weighing of evidence, vacillation and incompleteness. Under this view judgment is a defective experience which can only be avoided by the clarity of intuition.

Clearly this desire for intuition is a harking back to the desire for absolute certainty, a decision where no mistake can be made. However, it can uphold its separation from judgment only by producing a loaded definition of the thought process, as well as by making exaggerated claims for itself.

It is argued that thinking involves the creating of ideas and that these ideas then qualify existence: the formulation of the idea involves the separation of the predicate from the subject. It is argued that the process of thought is relational and not a direct experience, and it will therefore say something about experience but not what experience is. Intuition on the other hand is a non-relational experience and through it our consciousness somehow unites the subject and predicate together. It sees experience as it is and not in relational terms.

The thought process then is thought to be concerned with the manipulation of explicit relations mainly concerned with analysis and classification, and it has to make conscious and explicit judgments. If we accept that this is what the thought process is then there is something above the thought process. Yet why should this definition be accepted? Descartes argued long ago that while there is life the thought process never ceases. It may be, at times, muddled and disjointed but it always involves judgments — recent research has shown that there can be many different techniques of thought and learning.[9] Even to recognise an intuition we have to make a judgment as to whether or not it can be classed as an intuition, whether it is relevant, whether it is sensible, etc.

Oakeshott argues that experience is a form of thought and that thought is a collection of ideas. It follows that what is given in experience must also be a world of ideas. He believes we create a system of ideas in order that we can understand the world. Our attempt is to create order out of chaos. In a sense our aim in organising our ideas in this way is to create a world more satisfactory and understandable than the real world. Our ultimate aim then is coherence: the coherence of a given world of ideas.

However, if experience is a world of ideas which we ourselves have created and we always look at the world from within this system then is it ever possible to know the truth? Oakeshott argues that such a question is really meaningless because what is satisfactory to experience can be considered as true, and nothing except that which is true can be properly known, 'Without experience there can be no truth; without truth there can be no experience.'[10] We have already seen that experience is a system of ideas, and that our aim is to achieve coherence. It therefore follows that truth must be related to the system of ideas but we cannot say that a particular idea can be true as 'particular ideas are abstractions such as cannot be supposed to afford satisfaction in experience.'[11] What can afford satisfaction in experience is the whole, so the truth belongs to what is a whole. The criterion of truth then is the coherence of the world of experience. A world of ideas can be considered true when it is coherent. We cannot test the truth from the outside as it is not independent of our experience or our knowledge. We can only examine from the inside for coherence.

The same argument applies in the case of reality. There is not an independent reality and therefore we cannot test our knowledge by reference to that independent reality. Oakeshott states that arguments about an independent reality are making the assumption that knowledge and reality are separate entities. This he denies for he argues that knowledge must have its place in the real, and reality has to link with the universe of knowledge. If experience cannot be considered real then nothing can be real and nothing unreal, and if reality is separated from knowledge then it is nothing, and would be irrelevant. His conclusion is that reality and knowledge cannot be separated.

Oakeshott concludes, 'No separation is possible between reality and experience; reality is experience and nothing but experience. And since reality is always a world of ideas, reality is a world of ideas.'[12] Oakeshott points out that he is not arguing that the world is a world of mere mental events, for his notion that experience is a world of ideas recognises that when ideas are taken to be belonging to a world they have ceased to be just mental events. My experience is mine and my psychical state but it is not just mine. Reality is what 'we are obliged to think; and since to think is to experience, and to experience is to experience meaning, the real is always what has meaning, or is rational.'[13]

Reality and experience then are inseparable, and they form a world of coherent ideas. But they are not just any old ideas but a world of necessary or coherent ideas, ideas that I am obliged to think.

Oakeshott argues that our aim is to form a coherent world of ideas but that we in fact often fail to achieve this end, and a reason for this is that we turn away from the criterion of satisfaction which the process entails and begin to construct and examine 'a restricted world of abstract ideas.'[14] These restricted worlds or modes of experience are constructed as homogeneous and specific pictures not of part of the real world but of the whole of experience from the particular point of arrest.

These modes of experience are independent of each other, and each attempts to give a coherent view of the world, and in that sense is true for itself. The fact that they are independent implies that there cannot be a direct relationship between them, and that each world of ideas is a specific organisation of the whole of experience exclusive to itself. We therefore cannot speak of disputes or agreements between modes, and we cannot move in argument from one mode to another without committing a grave error. The arguments from one mode would be irrelevant to another. In fact, of course, many disputes do arise because of a failure to recognise that language from different modes of experience are being used.

Oakeshott points out that no limit can be put on the modes of experience that can be developed but that there are four obvious ones that have developed their own universal character and language. He calls these practice, science, history and poetry.[15] In the case of science we will examine the world under the category of quantity being mainly concerned with measurement, and attempt to develop a body of coherent ideas expressing this task, and also develop an appropriate specialised language in order to exchange these ideas. The mode will be autonomous in the sense that its truth will be related to the coherence of its own ideas, and that attempts to look at the world differently will be irrelevant to it. It will be independent *vis à vis* the other modes.

Notice what Oakeshott has done. As an idealist philosopher he has argued that our experience is a world of ideas, a necessary and coherent system of ideas; that there can be no reality that is separate to our experience and that truth must be related to the coherence of the ideas. He has also argued our aim (in fact he means man in his critical mood — as a philosopher) is to form a completely coherent world of ideas. But we are often turned from this task by the attractions of examining the world in an abstract way. We arrest experience and begin to examine experience from the point of view of different modes, and these different modes are independent and autonomous ways of examining the world.

Interpretative Frameworks

The theories that Michael Polanyi puts forward are in a number of respects the type of theories which Oakeshott would criticise. For instance, Polanyi argues that there is an independent external reality, and that the criterion of truth is whether our claim to have knowledge coincides with that reality. Unfortunately we can never be sure that it does so we therefore have to rely on our own beliefs about it. Oakeshott would argue that such a concept of reality is meaningless and irrelevant. If you cannot know it, if it is hidden from you, then how do you know that reality cannot be known. The argument is self contradictory, If we conceive of the word 'reality' meaning 'the whole of reality', an absolute concept, we cannot then argue that it is separate to our experience, as experience itself is part of reality — reality cannot be one thing amongst other things. Although Polanyi is an unorthodox realist and Oakeshott is an idealist they do nevertheless have a whole number of concepts in common which are particularly relevant to education. One of these is Polanyi's concept of the interpretative framework which is analogous to Oakeshott's modes of experience.

Polanyi, in examining the process of discovery in science, argues that we cannot conceive of the process taking place in a vacuum. It is not a random process where discovery is arrived at by accident but comes about within a certain interpretative framework. And he means by interpretative a group of systematic or coherent ideas to which we are committed and which we use to interpret and understand phenomena. In *The Study of Man*[16] he argues that all judgments take place within an interpretative framework, and can only be understood and estimated by reference to it. An interpretative framework is a way of looking at things but a way of looking at things in a way that will give stability to our perceptions. We fit things into a framework so that we can understand them and make judgments about them. Science for Polanyi is a sophisticated way of making judgments within a specialised interpretative framework but it is only a developed form of a process which all thinking animals use: to think is to make judgments. For example, a trout which snaps at an angler's fly. The trout is making a judgment, although an incorrect judgment, and the judgment is within a certain interpretative framework, and a framework which is appropriate for him in the circumstances. (An idea similar to Oakeshott's idea of being 'obliged to' think in a certain way.) Nevertheless it is possible that a wrong interpretative framework could be used: that the interpretative framework is only seemingly appropriate but in fact is not. He gives the example of young geese who accept a human being as their mother, and then proceed to identify other human beings as part of the flock. The geese are judging their experience in the right way but are using a wrong interpretative framework. The two errors are errors of thinking animals and can be distinguished from a pathological absence of any judgment which arises, for instance, when the appropriate part of the brain has been removed. We have in fact four possibilities in making a judgment: (1) An incorrect judgment in a correct interpretative framework; (2) A correct judgment in an incorrect interpretative framework; (3) A correct judgment in a correct interpretative framework; (4) An incorrect judgment in an incorrect interpretative framework. All these can be distinguished from a situation where no judgment takes place and no interpretative framework exists. (The case of animals with the appropriate part of the brain removed.)

Both Polanyi and Oakeshott recognise that to think is to make judgments, and that the making of judgments can only be understood by examining them in different frameworks of ideas. It does seem, however, that the Oakeshottian mode of experience is a wider concept than Polanyi's interpretative framework, and is more akin to the concept of a point of view. I will again take science as an example of a mode of experience.

In science we look at things from a limited point of view. Generally we look at things under the category of quantity and are mostly concerned with measurement. The world of ideas we create will be a world which is stable, uniform and common, and because of this it will be universal and communicable. Personal perceptions, although necessary in the process of discovery will be withdrawn in order to achieve this communicability, this public knowledge. The ideal is the mathematical language of measurement, which is the most stable and communicable. Indeed if it cannot be put in terms of mathematical relationships we can consider it non-scientific or at most pre-scientific. And from this it can be seen that physics must be considered the paradigmatic form of scientific achievement.

In looking at data from a particular mode of experience we use different interpretations to organise it. These different interpretative frameworks may themselves be 'incommensurable' with their own special language and concepts. Nevertheless it would seem to be the case that frameworks can be similar to those used in different modes of experience or viewpoints (making it even easier to make the mistake of sliding from one mode of experience to another in an argument). But the mode of experience will determine in a very general way what is relevant or not. For instance, science remains concerned with measurement and the finding of causal relations even if within this general approach we use different ways of looking at things (e.g. Newtonian and Einsteinian physics).

Normally relevant interpretative frameworks will be subsumed under particular points of view but it sometimes happens that a particular interpretative framework can attempt to take over a point of view, and the claim made that the use of a particular interpretative framework determines whether you are a historian, scientist, etc. For instance, Oakeshott spends a lot of time attempting to delineate what history is by ruling out certain approaches to it, so for him a Marxist historian would not be a historian, but a sort of historian/technologist who was using history for another purpose, to bring about revolution, and using illegitimately the concept of scientific laws taken from the scientific approach. In fact the Marxist example provides a good illustration of the attempt of an interpretative framework attempting to take over a discipline in history and sociology.

A Marxist will look at a historical situation from a Marxist interpretative framework. He will include in the framework a belief that in a social situation signs of a class struggle will be in evidence, and that the state will in all probability be an instrument used by the ruling class to maintain its power, that the state will have a parasitic element in it and will do things that will also benefit the bureaucracy. When an actual situation is examined evidence will be judged in accordance with this framework, and in the process will tend to confirm the validity of the approach. Conflict will be interpreted as class conflict, and legislative evidence will be found to confirm the Marxian hypothesis that legislation will be in the interests of the ruling class. If there is contrary evidence this will not be considered a direct challenge to the validity of the interpretative framework but as grounds for improving its sophistication. Certain *ad hoc* additions will be made which make the framework more flexible and coherent. Notice how this would be an anathema to an objectivist like Popper, as it would be protecting the hypotheses from falsification. We find Marx when examining the reign of Louis Philippe, King of the French,[17] copes with the problem that the whole of the bourgeoisie were not ruling, as they should be in orthodox Marxist theory, by calling the competing groups factions of the ruling class, and not by a declaration that they represented members of a different class, and, of course, he could not argue this as it would have destroyed the coherence of his position. More fundamentally Lenin copes with the problem that capitalism is not collapsing by developing his theory of imperialism.

Marxism then determines how the Marxist historian looks at history but has the further claim that it is the only way to look at history: that to be a historian one has to be a Marxist historian. A dispute can then arise as to what is the nature of the discipline.

Conclusion

Using the work of Oakeshott and Polanyi it has been argued that when we look at the world in an abstract way we are not looking at it as a concrete whole but through certain 'arrests of experience' or modes of experience which delimit the world and make us look at it in a certain way, for example, in science under the category of quantity. From within these general points of view we then attempt to organise it even further within certain clusters of ideas or interpretative frameworks. Our aim within the modes and within the frameworks is to achieve coherence, a completely stable world of ideas, and for Oakeshott coherence is the criterion of truth. Polanyi, in fact, accepts that the aim is to achieve coherence but argues that coherence is a criterion of stability not the truth. As a realist he has to argue the criterion of truth is the agreement of the ideas with reality but in fact, as he also argues that we can never be sure that an agreement with reality has been achieved, for practical purposes his criterion of truth is coherence. We could say for him coherence at least indicates that the truth has probably been achieved. The problem is of course, that coherence is never achieved and at certain points interpretative frameworks break down without leaving pointers for further development. Thus the clash of incommensurable frameworks.

This highly theoretical discussion seems to have great importance for education and certainly had considerable influence on both Oakeshott's and Polanyi's view of education. Thinking is making judgments and judgments arise from within different interpretative frameworks. We cannot conceive of a judgment being made without an interpretative framework. Education is in part the attempt to teach or rather show how judgments are made, as well as the initiation of children into the common culture. But under this analysis this now means initiating them into different ways of looking at the world. This is one of the reasons why Oakeshott, in fact, regards school education in such a limited way. He states:

> Learning to speak before one has anything significant to say; what is taught must have the qualities of being able to be learned without necessarily being understood . . . Or, it may be said, what is taught must be capable of being learned without any previous recognition of ignorance: we do not suddenly begin to learn the multiplication table because it suddenly dawns on us that we do not know the sum of nine eights, or the dates of the kings of England because we do not know when Edward I came to the throne: we learn these things at school because we are told to learn them.[18]

R. S. Peters in a generally favourable essay on Oakeshott criticises this approach as not 'defensible or necessary',[19] as a rejection of discovery methods, and as a failure to take note of the interests of each child. But the point Oakeshott is really making is related to the way we look at the world. Before we can show initiative or make discoveries we have to be shown our way round a discipline. We have to realise a discipline's potentialities and only then can we make adequate judgments. Education must partly consist of inculcating ways of looking at the world, and the development of the skill of making judgments and decisions within a discipline. Oakeshott calls this 'imparting' which includes the notion of learning from a master, learning by example. Polanyi likewise has a similar concept of a master/apprentice relationship. Aristotle also made a similar point when talking about moral decisions. The right decision was arrived at by the practised man of wisdom who was skilled in making decisions, and only he could perceive the right time, the right place, and right way to arrive at the appropriate decision for the occasion. A child's education is much like that of an apprentice where a whole lot of things have to be taken on trust. 'At school we are quite properly, not permitted to follow our own inclinations.'[20]

Notes

1. M. Oakeshott, *Experience and Its Modes*, (CUP, Cambridge, 1933).
2. M. Polanyi, *Personal Knowledge*, (Routledge, London, 1958), p. 175.
3. The examples are taken from J. M. Brennan, *The Open-Texture of Moral Concepts* (MacMillan, London, 1977).
4. Ibid, p. 29.
5. Oakeshott, *Experience and Its Modes*, p. 9.
6. Ibid, p. 10.
7. Ibid, p. 11.
8. Ibid, p. 16.
9. Cf. N. Entwistle & D. Hounsell (eds.), *How Students Learn* (University of Lancaster, 1975).
10. Oakeshott, *Experience and Its Modes*, p. 48.
11. Ibid, p. 48.
12. Ibid, p. 54.
13. Ibid, p. 55.
14. Ibid, p. 70.
15. In *Experience and Its Modes* he includes practice, history, and science. Poetry is included in his later writings.
16. M. Polanyi, *The Study of Man* (Routledge, London, 1959).
17. Cf K. Marx, *Eighteenth Brumaire of Louis Napoleon*.
18. M. Oakeshott, 'The Study of Politics in a University' in *Rationalism in Politics and Other Essays* (Methuen, London, 1962), p. 306.
19. R. S. Peters, 'Michael Oakeshott's Philosophy of Education' in P. King and B. C. Parekh (eds.), *Politics and Experience* (CUP, Cambridge, 1968), p. 45.
20. Oakeshott, *Rationalism in Politics*, p. 306.

3 TACIT KNOWLEDGE

Oakeshott and Polanyi have argued that thought involves constant judgments, for we always attempt to place information into a context we can understand. In fact we cannot make a clear distinction between the information we receive and our own judgments about it. Indeed information only becomes information when we assimilate it into our thought patterns, and begin to organise it in a comprehensible way.

We can attempt to understand this process in two different ways. We can either reflect on the nature of knowledge or reflect on how we acquire knowledge by the process of teaching and learning. Generally speaking Polanyi approaches an understanding by reflecting on the nature of knowledge and Oakeshott approaches it by analysing the actual process of teaching and learning. In this chapter Polanyi's reflections on the nature of knowledge are examined.

On Knowing Reality

As a realist Polanyi is not just concerned with the process of knowing but with the structure of reality itself. As we have seen he conceives of reality as an independent existence to ourselves. It remains the same whatever we believe about it. He argues that reality consists of not just appearances, the physics and chemistry of matter, but exists beyond that in a hierarchical structure. Traditionally it has been the practice to understand nature by an explanation which attempts to understand the reasons and causes of physical things, that is a causal explanation is given. However, Polanyi attempts to understand nature in what we can call its natural cohesion. In other words he is arguing that an attempt must be made to understand the patterns and coherence of nature by allowing our mind to 'flow-with' nature and not by imposing on it an artificial pattern of cause and effects. Two points are worth noting: the traditional approach gives us a restricted view of nature as a system of cause and effects but at the same time it does allow us to be artificially objective. We can at least test for cause and effects. The alternative approach of Polanyi looks for coherences and patterns in nature but does not allow the same sort of objectivity. There is no place for or possibility of conclusive tests, as we are looking for patterns and coherences. Tests can only provide indications that they are there.

Polanyi illustrates his concept of nature as a hierarchical structure analogously by looking at the structure of language:

> The first level, lowest of all is the production of the voice; the second, the utterance of words; the third, the joining of words to sentences; the fourth, the working of sentences into a style; the fifth and highest, the composition of the texts. The principle of each level operates under the control of the higher level.[1]

He indicates that in this illustration each level is subject to a dual control: by the laws that apply to its elements in themselves, and by the laws that form the comprehensive entity formed by them. He argues that this dual control is made possible because 'the principle governing the isolated particulars of a lower level leave indeterminate their boundary conditions for the control by a higher principle.'[2] For instance he indicates that voice production will leave open the combination of sounds to words, which is controlled by a vocabulary and a vocabulary will leave open the combination of words to form sentences which is controlled by grammar, and so on. As this is the case we cannot therefore account for the operation of a higher level by laws governing its particulars which form the next lower level. For example, 'you cannot derive a vocabulary from phonetics, and you cannot derive a grammar from a vocabulary.'[3]

As an analogy this example is designed to show that the levels of reality are open upward but not reducible downwards, that is, we cannot ultimately reduce reality to the physics and chemistry of matter. It also indicates that in attempting to understand this reality we must likewise grapple from one level of reality to the next, and that the open endedness of each level will lead us for ever onward towards a deeper understanding. A major point of Polanyi's argument then is that the structure of our comprehension is akin to the structure of reality itself, to that which is comprehended.

As can be seen from the language analogy a feature of the make up of reality are the factors of control and open endedness: order and freedom. Polanyi had been an eminent physical chemist, and his studies in chemistry and crystallography had indicated to him that there were two sorts of order: (1) an order which comes about through limits which are placed on the 'freedom of components, of molecules or cells: and (2) order that arises as full scope is given to their material interactions.'[4] The second type was more interesting. It was a spontaneous order which operated with a determinate framework, but was restricted but not determined by it. It is the type of order we find in crystal formations, which arises within a set of conditions but cannot be imposed on them. We can say that it is achieved through 'a natural equilibration of matter and energy.'[5] Polanyi also found a kind of spontaneous order in living organisms and speaks of it as the function of living mechanisms. This order has a basis in physical and chemical relations, but is not determined by them. It arises at 'the boundary condition left open by physics — chemical relations and develops structural or functional principles of its own.'[6] This, as can be seen, is a radically different theory to the one based on a mechanistic Newtonian framework, as Polanyi has a notion of a stratified universe where the different levels are coordinated with each other in a way that higher organisations spontaneously emerge. The higher organisms rest on a lower level of organisation without being determined by them. They are controlled in certain respects but not determined by them and rather put merely a limit on the sort of organisation that can emerge.

The same kind of order can be found operating in our perception, for instance, in the way we are able to assemble and integrate clues, in order to understand reality as a dynamic structure, an understanding which often collapses when we try to analyse our immediate understanding.

Polanyi argues that if we are to gain an understanding of reality we must 'indwell' within the clues of perception. He means by this that we cannot expect to gain an understanding of something we are not interested in. We have to immerse ourselves in it and make it part of ourselves. We become obsessed by it, and it is this obsession which puts us in a position to recognise the merging patterns. We do not create the reality but sometimes inadequately recognise its structure. The concepts we come up with after due consideration and criticism are, for Polanyi, not merely creations of our mind but are constructs directly related to reality.

This theory is really a psychological explanation of how we arrive at a discovery but he also attempts an analysis from a logical point of view. We can call this his theory of tacit integration.

The theory assumes that knowing has to be an act that involves personal judgment and commitment, and provides further reasons why knowing cannot be objective in the traditional sense. It is a theory about subsidiary and focal knowing, which he also sometimes calls proximal and distal knowing. We attend from one pole to attend to another. The psychological explanation Polanyi gives of this process is, in fact, closely akin to that of the Gestalt psychologists but is a more dynamic concept. He states:

> We may say, for example, that we know the clues of perception by dwelling in them, when we attend to that which they jointly indicate; and that we see the parts of the whole forming the whole by dwelling in the parts. We arrive thus at the conception of indwelling.[7]

We indwell in the clues of perception to give us a knowledge of the whole. This does not mean that we concentrate on the particulars and that this will give us a knowledge of the whole, as this in fact would prevent a pattern merging. What Polanyi is claiming is that we, in a sense, assimilate the particulars, '. . . we can say that when we make a thing function as the proximal terms of tacit knowing, we incorporate it into our body — or extend our body to include it — so that we dwell in it.'[8] He argues that by this process, by interiorising things, we begin not to view them as particulars but use them to attend to the comprehensive entity which they form. We, in a sense, forget about the particulars as such and use them to attend to the emerging pattern. And, as the Gestalt psychologists have pointed out, an attempt to reverse the process by concentrating on the particulars can make the new pattern disappear. However, as can be demonstrated by visual examples, we can continually switch back and forth from looking at the particulars and looking at the whole. What we cannot do is to see them as particulars and as a whole at the same time.

It in fact seems possible to discover a pattern in different ways. It is possible after a concentration on an apparently chaotic agglomeration of particulars for a pattern to emerge spontaneously. It is also possible for us to be led to perceive a pattern by having the elements of a pattern and its connecting links indicated to us. On the other hand it is also possible to consciously create patterns on apparent chaos (gestalten — bildung).

I want to examine these different possibilities and relate them to Polanyi's thought.

(1) We perceive certain facts, primary, aboriginal facts.[9] We build up concepts about these primary facts and our concepts are given the value of factual existence. That is we believe that the concepts we have are accurate constructs of reality. For us then these mental concepts are our way of understanding the primary facts, and for us they virtually are the facts. Already the process of organising chaos has begun, we have built up mental images or concepts of the primary facts, and in doing so we have isolated them from other things.

We may spontaneously perceive the relationships between them so that a pattern is created which ties the concept together into a comprehensive concept of them all or perhaps in part. Spontaneity in this case may be related to our previous experience, as a pattern may emerge which is analogous to other patterns we have perceived. It arises suddenly and comprehensively, and can be compared to a vision.

(2) We could be taught a comprehensive pattern, although it could be argued that a pattern perceived in this way may not be perceived in exactly the way the teacher expects. In order to teach a pattern a teacher would have to specify certain concepts about primary facts so that the pupil could understand how the pattern could be made to emerge, and then gradually indicate the connecting links between different facts in order to create the comprehensive picture. This uncertainty that the pupil has assimilated the facts in the way the teacher intends is analogous to the situation in science, where, when a theory is under consideration, we cannot be sure that it is being understood in the same way by all scientists. Hence the attempt to make scientific theories explicit and tie down their meaning, for instance, the continual attempt to mathematise all science. The teaching method this suggests, and which Polanyi in fact advocates, is that the pupil or rather apprentice should, as far as possible, be led to find his own patterns. That is the teacher should try and give the apprentice the skill to make his own discoveries within the existing

traditions of the enterprise. Eventually the apprentice scientist becomes able to perceive patterns without the help of the teacher, and becomes an independent and original scientist. Notice that the Polanyian scientist is an original scientist not just a Kuhnian puzzle solver.

The spontaneous emergence of a pattern comes about, so Polanyi claims, by trying to think about the facts, our concepts of the facts, as a whole until suddenly we perceive the connecting links, and see them, or rather understand them, as a whole. This is his main concept of discovery but there is a third possibility: a conscious attempt to create a pattern on seemingly disconnected facts.

(3) If a pattern does not spontaneously emerge we can sometimes create one by attempting to fit different patterns on the disconnected facts, or if this fails we can impose a pattern on them. An experienced scientist will have different experimental, mathematical, and statistical techniques which will sometimes bring about the emergence of a pattern. The pattern may arise not as a result of indwelling or commitment and a growing feeling of certainty but as a result of the application of certain techniques. It is possible, of course, to argue that this is accidental discovery but this would not be strictly true, as the scientist would be consciously using a number of techniques and approaches to the problem in the hope that some would bear fruit. The seeming contradiction of this possibility with the notion of indwelling can be weakened somewhat by an argument which states that a scientist will systematically use a series of techniques, and apply certain theories related to that particular field, with a fairly strong belief that some will bring about success. He will not be applying his theories and techniques at random, but will use his judgment and experience in deciding what is most likely to bring about the hoped for results. Generally, I think, this is not the Polanyian method of indwelling, although it may be a superficial level of it, as in this case it is unlikely that a scientist would develop the strong commitment to his theory which goes along with Polanyi's concept of discovery.

The notion of assimilating particulars, as we have seen, has another function within the Polanyian system. As well as being an aid, or rather a necessary step in the perception of gestalten, it enables one to forget about 'the particulars' and automatically use the knowledge of the whole which has been gained. We can give a practical example of this: we cannot learn to drive a car merely by reading an instruction book. We have to practise each operation until we become so skilled that it is second nature to us. Until we no longer think about what we should do but simply do it. Only when we have achieved this degree of competence can it properly be said that we can drive a car. However, even when we are a skilled exponent of the art of driving if we begin to think about each operation, that is when our attention moves from the whole to the particular, we will soon find ourselves crashing the gears, and our general technique falling apart.

In fact this example illustrates how we move from a knowing how to actually doing it, but Polanyi wants to use this argument with reference to scientific knowledge. In this case we use our knowledge of physical and chemical matter to give us an understanding of the lowest level of reality, we then use a knowledge of this level to rise to the next level and so on. We are able to do this because, as we have seen, each level of reality is open ended, and subject to a dual control: by the laws at its own level and by laws coming down from a higher level. We understand the lower level then by assimilating it or by making it part of ourselves, and we are in this way able to use it to recognise clues which will lead us to the next level. Polanyi is able then to fit his theory of knowing, which is a hierarchical concept, into his hierarchial concept of reality. The two theories are complementary to each other.

A Criticism of the Theory of Tacit Integration

Polanyi has argued that tacit integration is a process where we attend *from* one set of objects *to* another and that all knowing has this structure. It follows that subsidiary knowledge (proximal) is subsidiary in the sense that it is not attended to in itself but is used to attend to that which is focal (distal). That is you attend from it to something else. The focal or distal is the object we attend to, and we do attempt to describe it explicitly. Indeed it is our intention to examine it explicitly but it is not our intention to examine subsidiary knowledge explicitly, as within this process we take it as given and merely use it. Subsidiary knowledge then has a functional relationship to focal knowledge. In this sense subsidiary knowledge is implicit, but presumably if we do focus our attention on it we can make it explicit.

However, Polanyi wants to argue that there is necessarily a tacit dimension to all knowing, a dimension which therefore cannot be explained. It would seem to follow then that we cannot, in fact, make subsidiary knowledge wholly explicit, as we are just not aware of certain facets of our understanding. For example, we may not be consciously aware of our interpretative framework, or we may bring unrecognised values from our own peer group, and any attempt to make us aware can only lead to an infinite regress. It follows that every time we attempt to make something explicit we have to recognise that it will be surrounded by a whole body of assumptions of which we are not entirely aware. But it also follows that focal knowledge can never be made entirely explicit and that the same applies to subsidiary knowledge. This is why Polanyi sometimes states that his epistemology is that we know more than we can tell.

We can also explain Polanyi's analysis of indwelling and the perception of gestalten in this way. If we concentrate on the subsidiary, that is an attempt to make it explicit, we at the same time cannot use it to attend to something else — from it to something else. In fact we prevent tacit integration from coming about. In other words we destroy the functional relationship between subsidiary and focal knowledge.

There is a difficulty in this general theory because Polanyi wants to use this 'from-to' structure to explain the general process of knowing but it is questionable whether it can be used in this way. He wants to apply it to the purely perceptual, for example, 'How do we come to know a person's face?', and to the purely abstract or cognitive, for instance, 'How do we understand the works of Shakespeare?' or 'How do we give a meaning to the works of David Hume?'. To put it more technically he wants his model of knowing to apply to relationships in the real world, the perceptual field, and to relationships in the cognitive field, that is, relationships between propositional knowledge. An examination of the subsidiary or tacit in the former would involve an examination of the perceptual sensory elements of empirical experience, whereas in the latter it would take the form of an examination of, say, the categories by which Kant claimed we organised experience, or, perhaps the Oakeshottian modes of experience, or even Polanyi's own interpretative frameworks. Clearly in the former case we cannot think that the concept of tacit integration shows a logical structure of the 'from-to' process, as the relationship is between objects and not propositions, and logic, of course, is concerned with the relationships between propositions. Likewise, as we have seen in our examination of the process of tacit integration, an object or theory can be a 'to object' in one case and a 'from object' in another but it cannot be both at the same time. The conclusion must be that if we use Polanyi's concept of 'from-to' to reveal the process of tacit integration we cannot be revealing its logical structure. We are, however, 'following step by step the way in which someone whose intention it was to reveal what was tacit.'[10] In fact if we do use Polanyi's explanation of the 'from-to' process in this way, as an explanation of how we develop an understanding of tacit knowing rather than as a revelation of the logical structure of tacit knowing, then any tension between the perceptual and the cognitive case disappears. In practice, of course, we can not only remain in the same field — that is, move from the perceptual to the perceptual and the cognitive to the cognitive but can switch fields and go from the perceptual to the cognitive and vice versa. And sometimes one field can be subsidiary and at other times focal.

The Polanyian analysis then explicates the dynamic process of how knowledge is formed but this does not reveal its logical structure as Polanyi apparently believes.

Polanyi's gestalt-based psychology of discovery, and his explanation as to how we come to understand the hierarchical levels of reality, and reveal their structure, is startling and controversial. It is not only a rejection of the Newtonian mechanistic approach to science as a system of causes and effects but rejects the now orthodox neo-Kantian concept of science as the study of appearances and the attempt to explain these appearances by reference to universal laws. Polanyi at one point claims that he is a neo-Platonist where the knower is concerned with not just the physics and chemistry of matter and their explanation under the category of quantity, but with the essence of things. Not just with the 'lowest level' of reality but with an ascending hierarchy of reality that cannot be known through the senses but can be known through our intellectual and intuitive faculties. Thomas A. Langford in his paper 'Michael Polanyi and the Task of Theology'[11] even considered his approach and explanation of discovery as a visionary method of arriving at the truth. As we have seen to a certain extent he was justified in looking at the process in this way because of Polanyi's phraseology, its relationship to Gestalt psychology, and because of the claim that it revealed the actual structure of reality. Yet, in fact, Polanyi is not describing or even advocating a visionary method in the way that we would, for instance, describe Swedenborg's[12] method to be visionary. The vision is not a vision in the sense that it gives us a picture of reality. The word when used by Polanyi is used metaphorically. The new discovery is a vision in the sense that we have a very strong feeling of the nearness of reality. As our indwelling in our research deepens the feeling becomes stronger until we are virtually certain that we are revealing an aspect of reality, and, as Polanyi states, this deserves to be called a vision.

Much of the strange flavour in Polanyi's work comes about because Polanyi seems to be combining a realist concept about reality with an idealist framework. He is arguing that there is a separate reality which is independent to us but that we cannot effectively use this reality to test our theories. That our understanding is controlled by our categories of thought but our categories of thought are led on by a somehow hidden reality. And that in spite of the existence of an independent reality we can only rely on our own estimates of truth.

It does seem possible to explain the method of indwelling and the process of discovery in a more simple way, although in doing this we are at the same time challenging the notion that the method allows us to pass from the world of appearances to the Kantian world of things-in-themselves, or as Polanyi would say from the lowest level of reality to the hierarchical levels of reality beyond. Is not the scientist, as the philosopher, merely providing an interpretation of the available facts, an interpretation he believes to be the best, or the truth as Polanyi would say? Such an interpretation does, and is intended to provide a certain stability in seemingly disconnected facts and to provide clues for further interpretation. By arranging the facts into a theoretical framework the scientist is able to give an explanation of them. This task of arranging chaos into a pattern is by no means an easy process but an arduous one. It is an attempt to make sense of the facts by understanding them as a whole, and in such a way that all important elements amongst the facts are accounted for. Yet by its very nature the interpretation that is given cannot be on the same level as the facts themselves because at this lower level there is only chaos. One has to delve into the facts and try to find some connecting links or principles which can lead the way to some interpretation, and thereby help stabilise the chaos. By providing an interpretation one must be moving away from the basic facts, and this process of interpretation will probably continue as a good interpretation or theory should lead to further developments. Gradually, as new interpretations are built up on previous ones, we move even further away from the basic facts, and it may become extremely difficult to envisage the connecting links between them and the later or higher level interpretations. Nevertheless links there must be for, although at each stage one lifts the conclusion of an earlier level on to a new level, and in the process may change it into something that seems different, the new interpretation does remain an expansion of the earlier stage, and is necessarily related to it even though it is not immediately apparent that it is so.

If we accepted this simple explanation of Polanyi's concept of indwelling and process of discovery we would weaken the flavour of his work considerably. We would no longer need two world (world of appearances and beyond) or a multi-world theory but merely argue we are giving further interpretations of experience, and are building up concepts about the world available to our senses and these concepts cannot be said to make up another world, and indeed are meaningless unless we do relate them to this world of sense experience. It would also suggest that theories can be checked by reference to our original understanding of the phenomenal world. Furthermore it would withdraw some of the mystical flavour apparent in Polanyi's work — for instance, the miraculous spontaneous emergence of gestalten, and the need for us to be led to discovery by a benevolent spiritual reality. We would put the patterns and concepts, or interpretations, there by the power of our own mind (gestalten bildung). Nevertheless his theory does point out most vigorously that behind each piece of knowledge or explicit statement there lies a whole body of unexpressed, and sometimes inexpressible assumptions and beliefs.

Conclusion

Polanyi is trying to analyse the process of discovery. He argues that if we are going to gain success in the task then we must indwell in our research. It is only by doing this that we can begin to recognise the structure of reality, and begin to build up a commitment to what we see. This commitment heightens as we progressively understand the structure. In other words we begin to feel that our understanding of this reality is the truth, and eventually, after due consideration, we will claim that our understanding of this reality is the truth. In Polanyi's terminology this is our personal knowledge. Nevertheless in spite of this terminology personal knowledge can be no more than a belief to which we are very strongly committed, and for which we make truth claims. These beliefs are then used by us to develop further beliefs or theories, and to describe and even predict events in the actual world. If we are an original and mature scientist we can only rely on our own estimates of a theory's truth, although we may take note of the contrary arguments of other experts.

Polanyi, then, rather than proposing a logic of discovery, provides us with a description and a psychological analysis of how a scientist makes a discovery by an emotional immersion in his research. Yet the resultant commitment that the scientist has to his discovery cannot be considered a justification of its truth. At best it can provide an explanation as to why the scientist makes a claim his theory is true. This is why a scientist, when presenting a scientific paper, does not refer to the strength of his commitment but provides arguments and experimental evidence to support his theory. Some reasons in the public world of science are irrelevant, for instance, to state that he strongly believes in the validity of his theory because he has a strong feeling which he knows indicates its validity may be the case but is not part of the evidence the scientific community would take into account when judging a theory. They want arguments that can be corroborated. Arguments that can be examined for inconsistencies, and logical jumps, and experimental evidence that can be repeated.

From a teaching point of view Polanyi's arguments point to a number of things. For instance, his argument that discoveries will not be made unless one becomes immersed in one's research points out the need to develop powers of concentration. By the very process of indwelling one is actively looking for explanations with a mind concentrated and alive to possibilities. We should be actively looking for connections that will integrate phenomena and create a whole — a Gestalt picture. Yet his theory is more positive than that of Gestalt in that we do not wait passively for patterns to emerge but try and make them emerge. Interestingly the theory is not just an explanation, a description of how discoveries are made but is prescriptive in the sense that it tells us how discoveries can be made. It is stating that a good theory does not come about by a clever scientist throwing bright ideas out off the top of his head, theories to which he is not committed but can only come from a committed scientist who has gone through the process of indwelling in his particular research topic. It follows that if you want to become a good scientist, or good at anything, you must become obsessed with your work, and it also points out that allied to this obsession must be the necessary skills to obtain success. That is, one must become adept at the skills of one's work. You make them an extension of yourself. These skills include an understanding of the theories and concepts of one's discipline, and not just an intellectual understanding — a know that — but an understanding of how to use them to expand one's knowledge, of how they fit together, and how they can be used dynamically. In passing Polanyi is really challenging Gilbert Ryle's[13] 'know that' and 'know how' distinction, for proper knowledge always includes a know how element.

His arguments about the nature of subsidiary and focal knowledge point to the necessity to continually develop a wider area of understanding. In fact in conversation he put great stress on the need for a scientist or intellectual to expand his knowledge through voracious reading. This emphasis was not just to indicate that the intellectual life is a life of learning but because his theories indicated that the wider read one became the greater the potential area of one's tacit knowledge. Focal knowledge always arises from a tacit base, and the wider the tacit base the more likely analogies and ideas can emerge which can be used by the disciplined mind to formulate new theories and discoveries.

Clearly then part of the teaching task is to attempt to develop the art of concentration by providing material that will stimulate the pupil's interest, and with the hope that an interest in one area will flow over into other areas. Yet Polanyi is only advocating 'discovery teaching' in a limited sense for much teaching has to be authoritative and given to the pupil without attached criticism. A pupil has to be shown round a subject, and begin to appreciate it and understand it before he ever criticises it. Early criticism can, for a pupil, destroy a subject before it has got off the ground. For instance, I have attended a first year undergraduate class on Descartes where the teacher immediately launched into a destructive criticism of the Cartesian system, and the class ended with a pupil asking why on earth we should consider such a trivial and mistaken philosopher, whose arguments were so palpably false, and how on earth could he be considered a great philosopher!

However, although Polanyi puts great emphasis on the personal element in the gaining of knowledge with his concepts of indwelling, tacit integration, and commitment, and the aspects of teaching and learning I have mentioned are all related to this, there is the public element. How is this knowledge expressed, and how is it to be examined and understood by others? It is the problem of knowledge in its social context, for clearly, as I have pointed out, we cannot state from a rational point of view that this piece of knowledge is correct because I believe it to be so. Or, that I like it, so you must like it as well. It is a problem we will return to in a later chapter.

Notes

1. M. Polanyi, 'The Modern Mind: Its Structures and Prospects', lecture delivered at Bowdoin College, Brunswick, Maine, October 1964.
2. Ibid.
3. Ibid.
4. T.F. Torrance, 'The Open Universe and the Free Society', address given at the naming of the Michael Polanyi Seminar, University of Manchester, 11th November, 1978. Reprinted in *Convivium*, no. 7, Spring 1979.
5. Ibid.
6. Ibid.
7. Polanyi, *The Modern Mind*.
8. M. Polanyi, *The Tacit Dimension* (Routledge and Kegan Paul, London, 1966), p. 16.
9. A term used by William James meaning basic facts before we have developed any concepts about them.
10. Rom Harre, 'The Structure of Tacit Knowledge', *The Journal of the British Society for Phenomenology*, vol. 8, no. 3 (October, 1977).
11. *Journal of Religion*, vol. XLVI (1966).
12. Cf. *Heaven and Hell* (Swedenborg Society, London, 1958).
13. *The Concept of Mind* (Hutchinson, London, 1949).

4 TEACHING AND LEARNING

Michael Oakeshott conceives of education as the process of initiating each new generation into the cultural heritage of their community. However, this initiation is not a mere process of indoctrination, where a child is moulded into a pattern which is useful for society. The process gives the child a considerable degree of freedom to develop his own talents but nevertheless this freedom will lie within what Oakeshott calls 'circumstances of direction and restraint'.[1]

Oakeshott sees the process as the gradual participation of the pupil into the different 'conversations of mankind'. The pupil begins to recognise that there are different varieties of human utterances and he starts to practice them himself. He begins to understand and work within the different modes of experience.

There is the problem here that a pupil may become confined within one mode of experience, for, as we have already seen, Oakeshott believes that each mode of experience — science, history, poetry, etc., — will have its own language, and a literature which is peculiar to itself. It is partly in an attempt to deal with this problem that he demarcates between what we can call different levels of education, although we could also call them different types of education.

Oakeshott sees education as a two way process where pupils have an 'initiation into . . . a civilisation and in doing so discover our own talents and aptitudes and use them'.[2] In practice this means the child is initiated into the different languages and literature — modes of experience — of civilisation. At this point the pupil is hesitant in his use of the language so that much of the material he comes across and assimilates he cannot use. He therefore has to take much on trust in order to build up background knowledge for later use. Oakeshott sees this period where the pupil absorbs the traditions of civilisation and develops the different skills to participate in the different conversations, as the period of school education. It is a period when the pupil does not really see where he is going but does develop the talents necessary to assert his own independence and freedom of action.

A period where the pupil absorbs and the teacher feeds.

The argument that Oakeshott develops, in spite of its exotic language, is straightforward. Early education has to be an initiation into the use of language and in techniques of communication with others. It gradually develops into the more specialised use of language and argument as the pupil is introduced to the different literatures. This is a long process as the pupil feels his way towards a competence that may give him a degree of independence. But it is a competence that can only be gained under the guidance and restraint of the teacher.

By its very nature education has to be authoritative as the pupil has neither the skill nor the knowledge to act on his own. Freedom lies not in the exercising of one's mind at random but through the controlled application of it, as one begins to feel confident within a mode of experience. However, it is at this point that school education ends so that under our present educational system the vast majority of pupils take no further steps into an understanding of our cultural heritage. In fact very few pupils reach this stage.

Two other forms of education follow which Oakeshott designates vocational and university education. In vocational education the pupil acquires a literature which is particularly relevant to a particular skill, or rather he acquires the literature and the skill. It is also a skill which is directly relevant to the contemporary world. In a way Oakeshott's account of this sort of education is more an account of craft training. The pupil learns a specific body of information and knows how to use it but he need not have a deep understanding of the principles that lie behind the craft. He has the know how and the skills, and has the rule-of-thumb method at his fingertips. He is essentially a technician. Oakeshott, then, conceives of vocational education as a training in the received knowledge of a subject, its literature, and an acquisition of the necessary skills to make use of this knowledge. We could call it an education in the literature rather than the language of a subject, for the vocationally trained pupil does not innovate but practises. He is the man who wires the house not the person who formulates principles of electricity in the first place.

This concept of vocational education is inadequate but useful for Oakeshott, as it allows him to make a demarcation between vocational and University education. University education is an education in the languages of the modes of experience. At this level of education we are no longer concerned merely with received information but also in developing the information itself, and in attempting to recover what has been lost and in following intimations that may lead to innovations. In other words education, at this stage, is not just the passing on of information which has to be assimilated by the pupil but is concerned with a language that can be used, explored and played around with for its own sake. For instance, the pupil no longer just reads history but becomes an historian. This means that he does not just read the literature but undertakes his own research, and uses the literature not as a tool for practical use but as a means of understanding the activity of being an historian.

When Oakeshott turns to the question of how civilisation is passed on from generation to generation he develops a distinction between what he calls technical and practical knowledge. Technical knowledge is the sort of knowledge you can find in a textbook, where the knowledge is put into a form of rules and principles. These rules can be memorised and the attempt made to put them into practice. Yet this attempt can never be entirely successful, as one cannot become an expert by reading an instruction book. One cannot become an expert golfer by reading a golfing manual or even by carefully following the diagrams in the manual. This leads to Oakeshott's analysis of practical knowledge. This sort of knowledge cannot be formulated as a set of rules. It is concerned with actually doing something, and is the sort of knowledge that can only be shown. Oakeshott states:

> It exists only in practice, and the only way to acquire it is by apprenticeship to a master — not because the master can teach it (he cannot) but because it can be acquired only by continuous contact with one who is perpetually practising it.[3]

In order to explain this distinction from the point of view of the teacher Oakeshott first of all points out that he considers the activity of teaching as a deliberate activity, which has the intention of initiating a pupil into an aspect of civilisation. However, in order for this to be achieved there must be a pupil who is ready to receive the communication. He 'is a learner known to a teacher'.[4] Oakeshott then produces a model of the master and apprentice, the sage who in a sense leads the pupil to a participation in human life — into a civilisation. From a teaching point of view the relationship is even closer than this for the teacher concentrates on his pupil, and the initiation he undertakes is carefully thought about and ordered, and put into an appropriate form for transmission. The teacher's aim is not just to pass on information or the planting of a seed that may later grow but the tremendous aim of leading the pupil into a civilisation. To set the mind on an interest that will grow and to put the pupil on his first steps towards making deliberations and judgments of his own.

Oakeshott points out in passing that this provides a solution to the dilemma as to whether learning is to be understood as acquiring knowledge, or to be regarded as the development of the personality of the learner. Or, from the teaching point of view, whether teaching is concerned with initiating a pupil into an inheritance of human achievement, or whether it is designed to enable the pupil to make the most of himself. The reason why it solves the dilemma is that a pupil learns to make the most of himself by living in the world of human achievement. Yet the teacher should not merely pass on and initiate the pupil into what at the present time is recognised as human achievement. He should not be solely concerned with modernity but with the passing on of knowledge of the whole of the human inheritance. After all there is no reason to believe that what is fashionable has the most value. Indeed, as far as possible he should 'release his pupils from servitude to the current dominant feelings, emotions, images, ideas, beliefs and even skills . . .'[5]

Oakeshott indicates that this may seem a prodigious task for the teacher for the inheritance is complex, unfinished, ambiguous, and sometimes confused. It is not a carefully woven package of assured worth but nevertheless does contain everything that is of value and has to be 'the ground and context of every judgment of better and worse.'[6] What is handed on, of course, and learned and understood 'are thoughts and various expressions of thoughts'.[7]

Skills, Abilities and Judgments

What is being developed in the process of teaching and learning are the pupil's abilities, for knowledge in fact constitutes a number of abilities, and every complex ability is itself a manifold of simple abilities. Oakeshott points out that when an ability is recognised as an ability to do or make something, and has a high degree of physical movement, we will usually call it a skill. For instance, boxing, playing football and digging straight trenches are all skills and are a manifold of simple skills — for example boxing includes the ability to move one's feet quickly without losing one's balance, to react quickly to another person's moves, to punch correctly, and so on. We sometimes extend the concept of a skill to other activities which are not so obviously physical: a skilful chairing of a meeting, or a skilful performance of a piano concerto with the suggestion that one needs to be skilful to be great but that by itself it is not enough. We then begin to talk of abilities when we refer to performances that are not so obviously physical but rather mental — for instance, the ability to give a rousing speech, and the complex abilities to be an engineer, a farmer, a teacher, or a Greek scholar.

The concept of 'abilities' includes the notion of knowing and doing. It is an awareness of having a power to do certain things: the power (ability) to design overhead cranes, or the ability to decide on and sow certain crops. What we know is an equipment which enables us to do certain things but one ability cannot be assimilated with another ability: to have the ability to understand an explanation is distinct from having the ability to use that explanation, for example, understanding an explanation as to how an engine works and what is the fault as distinct from having the ability to mend a faulty engine.

Oakeshott argues that these abilities are conjunctions of 'information' and 'judgment'. Information is made up of facts, which can be itemised, and intellectual artefacts, and is impersonal. It can be found in such things as textbooks, dictionaries and encyclopaedias. However, the real importance of information lies in the fact that it provides 'rules or rule-like propositions relating to abilities'.[8] Each ability will have its rules which will be contained within a piece of knowledge we call information. For instance, pieces of information that tell us 'razors are sharp' or tell us what ingredients we need in order to concoct a certain dish. These rules or rule-like propositions can be related to knowledge in two different ways: (1) They can be items of knowledge that have to be known in order to perform, for example, to send morse messages you need to know morse equivalents of the letters of the alphabet. (2) They can constitute 'the criterion by means of which a performance may be known to be incorrect'⁹, e.g., rules of grammar are used to tell you whether the performance of a speech act was correct but they cannot be used to tell you whether the performance was a good one. Oakeshott also points out that there is also a third rule-like proposition which we call a principle. They provide the 'underlying rationale' of a performance, for instance, in the case of moral conduct we can say that good moral conduct exhibits the ability to behave well. A possible principle could be Aristotle's principle of the mean which tells you not to do things to excess but just to the right amount. It is really telling you what goes on in moral conduct but it does not give you a piece of knowledge which tells you how to act morally or gives you criteria which tell you whether a particular performance of a moral act is correct or incorrect. It rather gives an explanation of what is going on in moral activity.

This is the information side but if an ability is to emerge it has to work in conjuction with judgment. An ability then consists in having information and making judgments or in 'knowing that' and 'knowing how'. By the word judgment Oakeshott means partly the tacit component of knowledge that cannot be formulated into rules or rule-like propositions, and therefore cannot be given as information. This type of tacit knowledge, Oakeshott claims, is an ingredient of all genuine knowledge. Judgment then is not just a partner in a skill but more particularly in abilities connected to mental operations, for instance, the connoisseurship of the art critic, the feel of the translator. It is also not merely knowing how to apply the rules given in the information part of knowledge but knowing how to do it with finesse and artistry or, as Oakeshott sometimes calls it, with style. He develops this point in an illuminating passage.

> The rules of art are there, but they do not determine the practice of the art, the rules of understanding are there, but they do not themselves endow us with understanding. They set limits — often telling us only what *not* to do if we wish to speak on any of the languages of our civilisation; but they provide no prescription for all that must go in the interval between these limits.[10]

Information and judgments are different components of an

ability but the components are not distinct but are integrated together. This means that we cannot teach them separately. To give information successfully means that we must also give an understanding of that information and the ability to judge. However, we cannot teach the ability to judge without also teaching something to judge. Nevertheless this does not mean we can teach information and the ability to judge in the same way, although it does suggest we should not, and indeed cannot, have information classes and judgment classes. Oakeshott points out that the distinction between information and judgment is also a distinction between different ways of communicating, and arises from reflecting on teaching and learning rather than on the nature of knowledge. Under this approach teaching then becomes a twofold task of communicating information, which he calls 'instructing', and communicating judgment, which he calls 'imparting'.

The teacher, under his instructor's hat, introduces to his pupils a whole array of facts that may have no immediate significance. He has to decide which part of civilisation's inheritance is to be transmitted, and has to organise it in such a way as to make it readily available to his pupils, and of interest to them as well. The teacher, at this stage, does not introduce his pupils into 'modes of thought', but to arbitrarily designed subjects which make up a curriculum. Nevertheless the subjects do allow the facts to show their rule-like character, and indicate how they can be used as tools in doing, or making or understanding. The teacher, then, should try and lift the facts out of their inertness. He also wants his pupils to attempt to reorganise the information into forms different to that in which it was first acquired, as in that way they are themselves destroying the inertness of the facts.

The teacher must also impart judgment. It can be seen that the pupils begin to exhibit judgment when they begin to recognise that information must be used, and realise that certain things can be irrelevant to the achievement of specific tasks. They begin to use the facts as tools to do, and make, and understand, and perhaps explain in the mode of thought which is 'behind the information'. This imparting of judgment, as we have seen, cannot be a separate task on the part of the teacher but has to be a by-product of the process of instruction. Oakeshott claims it can only be achieved if the information, and rule-like propositions that go along with it, are related to concrete situations. The teacher not only imparts skills in judgment and the necessary intellectual apparatus that goes along with good judgment, for instance, doubt, concentration, disinterested curiosity, honesty, etc. — the intellectual virtues. He above all imparts the skills of listening, getting into the mind of the writer, understanding the nuances of the argument. Oakeshott writes: 'We may listen to what a man has to say, but unless we overhear in it a mind at work and can detect the idiom of thought, we have understood nothing.'[11]

The art of judgment can only be passed on through practice. It is a way of doing something and not information on how to do it, and therefore can exist long after the information has been forgotten. It can therefore become rusty but itself can never be forgotten.

Criticisms and Conclusions

I now wish to look at some criticisms of this distinction between 'instructing' and 'imparting'. Probably the major critical appraisal of Oakeshott's writing on education comes from R.S. Peters in his article 'Michael Oakeshott's Philosophy of Education'.[12] The criticism is twofold: a criticism of Oakeshott's concept of judgment, and a rejection of the notion that we cannot become an expert self-taught practitioner. A rejection of the notion that to become a master we have to be apprenticed to a master. I will discuss this notion within my consideration of the different concepts of judgment.

Peters argues that Oakeshott uses the word judgment in at least three different senses:

(a) It is used in the idealist sense to apply to a situation when a concept or rule is applied to a particular case. For instance, in order to recognise that a blotch is red one needs judgment, and to recognise that the red blotch is a leaf one needs further judgment. Likewise, to recognise that someone is fitting an engine together incorrectly one also needs judgment. This is a very general sense of judgment and one that Oakeshott often uses. However, Peters asks the question whether this sort of judgment would need to be imparted by a teacher. He argues that it would not:

To be able to perceive or think is to be able to use concepts, and learning a concept involves both learning the rule which binds together the instances and learning by examples that count as instances . . . But this process of producing an example to teach a concept or a rule is the most typical case of instruction.[13]

Yet if the child is then able to exhibit the skill of recognising instances and exemplifications of the general rule we could say we had imparted some ability to judge to him. However, Peters argues that the necessity of imparting judgment would not necessarily be involved, 'though, at some stage, the use of examples would be necessary, the example of the teacher would not. After all, a great deal of instruction of this sort can be carried out by a teaching machine'.[14]

Peters' point here is that once an early skill has been picked up, for instance, the skill of using language, then a great deal of judgment can be developed by mere instruction.

I do not see how this provides a successful criticism of Oakeshott's position. For instance, say a teaching machine gives you certain rules for working out mathematical equations. The machine then provides certain exemplifications of this, and works through the manoeuvres one needs to make in solving the equations, and then gives you the answers. Eventually the machine just gives you the answers, and perhaps may then go through the workings to demonstrate what you should have done — most reasonable text books will also do this. Once the pupil has learned how to apply the rules he begins, by following the instructions, to become skilful in applying the rules and solving the equations. The pupil, it appears, has been instructed into how to make the necessary judgments to arrive at the right answer. Oakeshott would surely argue that this is not so. The pupil has been instructed in what the rules are and has been instructed in the manoeuvres one should make if one wants to get the right answer. However, he has acquired himself the necessary judgment to work out the equations. He has within himself the potentiality to make judgments and this is led on in the right direction by the novel teaching machine. The pupil in a sense is self taught and has developed his own judgment.

The answer to this could be yes but the fact nevertheless remains that the situation is of a teaching machine and a pupil, and the pupil has acquired judgment while the machine has instructed. No 'imparting' has taken place, for we cannot talk of the child imparting to himself, therefore the instruction must have been instrumental in bringing about judgment.

It is possible to provide an answer to this point by arguing that information and judgment are really inseparable and that in all we undertake we make judgments. We can for analytical purposes make a distinction between them but the distinction is artificial, and likewise the distinction between instructing in information, and imparting judgment is also artificial. In fact the teacher by instructing cannot help imparting judgment, and this is why Oakeshott argues the two cannot be undertaken separately. The point of Peters' criticism seems to be that imparting and instructing can be undertaken separately, and that we can instruct people in how to make judgments. Yet in formulating rules we are already indicating an element of judgment and the element of judgment is partially revealed by the exemplifications of their application. There is also judgment in determining what are correct examples. The teaching machine does not make the judgments itself but is an intermediary in passing on the judgments already made in producing the rules, giving the exemplifications, and working out the solutions.

(b) Peters argues that the paradigm case of a more specific sense of judgment is the type of task performed by a judge. He has to meet a solution where a whole lot of rules may apply to a certain set of facts but he has to sort out what rule actually applies. Similar sorts of judgments are also involved in diagnoses, in deciding how to impress one's boss, etc. Judgment in this sense is essentially a term of approval, whereas we do not really use it as a term of approval if we use judgment in the first sense, the general idealist sense where a concept or rule is applied to a particular case. Peters argues: 'The fact is that we do not normally use the word "judgment" for the straightforward cases of applying rules or using information. We reserve it for the special cases where applying rules or interpreting information presents a problem.'[15]

Peters then asks the question whether judgment in the second value-laden sense has to be learnt by a master/apprenticeship relationship. He claims that Oakeshott argues that it can only be learnt by this method, and furthermore this is the burden of his political and educational writings, where he contrasts this way of developing judgment with formalised instruction or the use of manuals and guides.

I want to argue that this is not the case as can be shown by an examination of Oakeshott's general position. He argues in *Experience and Its Modes* that thought is judgment 'where there is meaning or significance there is judgment' and, 'No separation is possible between reality and experience, reality is experience and nothing but experience. And since reality is always a world of ideas, reality is a world of ideas.'[16]

He concludes from this that reality is what, 'we are obliged to think; and since to think is to experience, and to experience is to experience meaning, the real is always what has meaning, or is rational'.[17]

Experience is mine, and my psychical state but it is not just mine, as it is an understanding of what has meaning and is therefore rational. But clearly we can develop this judgment by reference to an instruction book. We can, for instance, develop some sort of skill at golf by simply following an instruction book and trying the suggestions made in the instruction book. Many people teach themselves to drive a car reasonably well without following a master. Peters is certainly correct in arguing that the self-taught person can develop a considerable amount of skill or judgment without needing a master. His argument is then that to have a master may be the best way of learning but is not essential.

The same argument I used previously can cope with some of this criticism. In learning from an instruction book one begins to recognise the judgments made in arriving at the rules. One uses one's own judgment to recognise the meaning lying behind the rules. Yet in learning to drive a car from scratch, as many people did after the car was first invented, without an instruction book, one learns by trial and error and by recognising the limitation provided by the mechanical nature of the car. Or if one was mechanically minded one can recognise beforehand what one would have to do before one could drive a car, and then simply practice it. One becomes proficient by teaching oneself. The general force then of Peters' criterion would hold.

However, I do not think Oakeshott is really arguing that you cannot have a self-taught cook, or hunter, or golfer who can achieve a considerable degree of proficiency, although it is certainly the case that he seems to be arguing this. Nevertheless it is not entailed by his original concept of judgment as set out in *Experience and Its Modes*, for to think is to make judgments. Another example of the development of judgment without a master/apprenticeship is when one learns in a group of peers. For instance, one can learn to wrestle, develop tricks, recognise the need for balance, etc., just by wrestling with a friend. Peters also points out that one can be taught to be highly expert by a person who himself is not an expert (Oakeshott actually argues this himself). Clearly then judgment can be imparted by people who are not masters or developed by oneself.

However, this argument does not destroy the thrust of Oakeshott's point. His argument is that as we are introduced to some of the contents of the modes of thought found in the heritage of civilisation, and as we become adept at learning the language, it becomes essential that we follow someone who knows what he is doing. For instance, with the highly specialised language of science and the complicated techniques that go with it, as well as the specialised forms of argument and presentation, it becomes essential that the pupil is led on by a master. In the case of science, for example, he is in a sense apprenticed into the community of scientists and shown round it by recognised experts, and hopefully he will eventually become an independent scientist. As a pupil develops his education the need for a master becomes increasingly important. The self-taught can get so far but, as the modes of thought become more complicated they are liable to fail. Indeed, if even at an earlier stage the pupil is not led on by a master it is likely that he will never achieve the necessary background knowledge to participate successfully in a mode of thought.

The imparting of judgment then is the major part of the teacher's role. It shortens the time a pupil may spend in achieving efficiency, and makes it far more likely that the pupil will eventually become a connoisseur. Oakeshott is not, as Peters suggests, sneering at the self-made man but saying he would have done a lot better if he had been educated properly, and wasted far less time.

(c) Peters also points out that Oakeshott often refers to the 'style' of the performer. Oakeshott means by this not just individual acts of judgment but the recognition of an individual intelligence at work in every act of judgment. Peters argues that Oakeshott 'seems to conflate together the possibility of detecting it in another and the possibility of acquiring it from another. But the two do not necessarily go together.'[18] He gives examples of when they do not, for instance, Wittgenstein's style of philosophy which can be disliked as against the importance of some of his insights. He points out that Oakeshott apparently uses the word 'style' as a sign-approval associated with desirable traits.

I again think that Peters has missed the point of the argument. Oakeshott has argued that by 'style' he means the recognition of an individual intelligence at work in every act or judgment. The point he is making is that without a proper understanding of the style of a person performing we will be unable to grasp entirely the meaning of that performance. For instance, if a person writes with heavy irony it is necessary to recognise this before one can really recognise the meaning of what he is writing. It is true that one could say that this is his irony and that this is what he means but what he means can only be understood by taking into account the irony.

It seems then that the position of Oakeshott and Polanyi are in a number of respects complementary. Oakeshott concentrates on how knowledge is going to be taught, and both emphasise the necessity for the pupil to be introduced to a specialised language in different modes of thought. Both also emphasise the need for the master/apprenticeship relationship as an almost necessary condition for a pupil to achieve this task. However, Polanyi provides a further theory about how knowledge is acquired by the knower and how it is used. Indeed he begins to do what Peters claims Oakeshott does not. He begins to dig into the uncharted regions of social learning. It is to the development of knowledge in a social framework that I now turn.

Notes

1. M. Oakeshott, 'The Study of Politics in a University' in *Rationalisation in Politics and Other Essays* (Methuen, London, 1966), p. 304.
2. Ibid. p. 304.
3. *Rationalism in Politics and Other Essays*, p. 11.
4. M. Oakeshott, 'Learning and Teaching' in R.S. Peters (ed.), *The Concept of Education* (Routledge and Kegan Paul, London, 1967), p. 160.
5. Ibid. pp. 161-2.
6. Ibid. p. 162.
7. Ibid. p. 163.
8. Ibid. p. 165.
9. Ibid. p. 165.
10. Ibid. p. 169.
11. Ibid. p. 175.

12. R.S. Peters, 'Michael Oakeshott's Philosophy of Education' in P. King and B.C. Parekh (eds.), *Politics and Experience* (CUP, Cambridge, 1968).
13. Ibid. p. 53.
14. Ibid. p. 54.
15. Ibid. p. 55.
16. Oakeshott, *Experience and Its Modes*.
17. Ibid.
18. Peters, *Politics and Experience*, p. 57.

5 THE SOCIAL CONTEXT OF KNOWLEDGE

So far we have considered the acquisition of knowledge as very much a personal thing. We have been concerned with the individual, and his ability to learn and eventually become an innovator. Yet clearly the individual is working within a social framework, and the claims he makes to knowledge are claims that the knowledge he possesses is a form of public knowledge: that it is objective knowledge and that other people should accept it as such. Michael Polanyi has made a study of these claims and their acceptance or rejection by the scientific community. In this chapter I will therefore analyse these arguments in order to illustrate how knowledge is accredited in the paradigm example of a professional and intellectual community. The analysis also points to the fact that the skills necessary for an effective functioning in such a community are far wider than at first appears. I will return to this point in the later chapter 'Argument and Persuasion'.

Polanyi has argued that it is the individual scientist who must make a discovery and eventually make a truth claim for his theory, but quite obviously his own commitment to a theory cannot automatically guarantee its acceptance. Before a theory can be considered to be part of scientific knowledge it has to be accepted by the scientific community as a whole. And as Polanyi has argued, as it is not possible to verify or falsify a theory only one alternative remains. A theory must be judged by the consensus of opinion within the scientific community.

The scientists will not have the discovery scientist's commitment to a theory but will use much of the same criteria in judging the theory: its systematic relevance, internal consistency, and beauty. They will also consider another major factor, and that is how far the discovery fits into the general framework of science. Polanyi states:

> Very little inherent certainty will suffice to secure the highest scientific value to an alleged fact, if only it fits in with a great scientific generalisation, while the most stubborn facts will be

set aside if there is no place for them in the established framework of science.[1]

A consensus of opinion about a theory can be formed, so Polanyi argues, because in the 'Republic of Science' there can be found the overlapping of labours. A scientist may know one per cent of all scientific knowledge, another whose work is near to his overlaps, and a joint authority is exercised in the overlapping area. This phenomenon is continued throughout the scientific community until a network of knowledge is formed and controlled by the combined authority of the members of the community. The individual scientist submits himself to the authority of his peers but at the same time will exercise a certain amount of authority himself. He will have some authority where his sector overlaps with others, and complete authority in his own sector where it does not.

The Republic then is controlled by an organic, general authoritative structure, and its authority is shared by all mature scientists. It is organic because all scientists are bound together by a mutual faith in the existence of external reality, and each attempts to be instrumental in serving the community by producing discoveries. The community has of necessity two conflicting elements. It is authoritative, and thereby creates a certain amount of conformity, but at the same time needs to allow individual initiative. Initiatives do not and cannot come from the community as a whole but from the mature scientist with his personal contact with reality.

Polanyi argues that the aggregate of individual initiatives on the part of the mature scientists creates a spontaneous order which is able to exist because of the coherence of science. He means by this that spontaneous co-ordination can come about because of the systematised nature of science, which allows the scientist to attempt to relate each new discovery to the systematic ideas of science. The system of knowledge is automatically used by the mature scientist to judge a theory. However, the possibility of acquiring and then using this knowledge originally arises because of the faith the scientist has in the existence of external reality. It is this faith, and the confirmation of the faith by the gaining of knowledge, which ultimately gives coherence to science.

He argues that this process of spontaneous co-ordination although not perfect, as it can make mistakes, does produce the best possible results. And the medium for this co-ordination is the instant publicity which is given to the results of research so that an immediate judgment is made possible. This spontaneous co-ordination of knowledge allows a consensus to arise, and this way of controlling the development of science is the only way possible. Independent research activities are guided and controlled by scientific opinion. It can be considered a polycentric system of mutual co-ordination and is the only way to control science because of the nature of science itself. Science is the attempt to understand an external reality which has an independent existence to ourselves. The reality can only be understood by our intuitive faculties and in order for them to come into play the scientist needs to be passionately committed to the traditions and values of science and to the search for reality. When a discovery is made he needs to be very strongly committed to its contents before he submits it to the community for their judgment. Scientific research then is an intensely personal act and this necessitates the scientist choosing his own research. Nothing must come between the scientist and his personal contact with external reality or discovery will be minimal. He achieves his discovery by the process of indwelling and any interference can only weaken or destroy the passionate commitment which grows through indwelling. Science then has to be autonomous and it cannot be controlled from the outside. It exists for its own sake and not for utilitarian purposes.

Only when the scientist has finally decided on the truth of his discovery does he submit it to the community for appraisal, and its possible acceptance into the general body of scientific knowledge. He 'asserts his independence by obeying the dictates of his own conscience'[2] but his obedience to his conscience means that he rigorously checks his discovery before submitting it to the community. The rigorously tested theory will only be put before the community if the discovering scientist is convinced of its truth. His conscience will not allow him to do so if he thinks it is something less than the truth. The members of the community will then judge the discovery by their own knowledge, and for Polanyi they can judge it by nothing else as he has denied the possibility of impersonal conclusive tests. We can say that it will be judged by the visions of reality that have already been received and accepted by the scientific community as knowledge. As each scientist is himself bound by his conscience to reveal the truth the judging scientists are bound to hold strictly to that which has already been revealed as the truth. The new theory will have to fit into theories that have already been accepted. It is not an arbitrary way of judging a theory but a reasonable method of judging the truth of a theory by comparing it with knowledge one already possesses.

The decision as to the worth of a theory can only be a conservative judgment and cannot be too radical or speculative. If it was then it would be an indication that the community was losing faith in that which it had already revealed, or that the consciences of its members were weakening. Change then can and does come about but it is continuous with the past, and arises because of the intimations of future discoveries which are contained in the present accepted theories.

Three confusing strands of thought seem apparent in the argument so far. Polanyi seems to be arguing that the individual scientist can perceive the truth; that the community judges a new theory by a consensus of opinion but as he compares this to a Rousseaunian General Will[3] he is also suggesting that it reveals the truth; and that the real truth is in accordance with external reality. The blanket term 'the truth' seems unable to cope with the distinctions which evidently exist between the three different truths. The confusion can be explained because Polanyi sometimes uses the term in a psychological sense, for instance, the scientist produces a theory which he believes is true. This is merely saying that the truth for the scientist is that which he believes is the truth. He cannot accept something which he does not believe as the truth, therefore the truth for him must be what he believes. Again the truth for the scientific community is that which it believes to be true. The members judge a theory by that which they believe to be true, for obviously they will not judge it by that which they consider to be false. The main criterion in doing this is whether or not the new theory fits into their jointly held beliefs. However, the real truth, we can say the philosophical truth, is that which is in accordance with reality but this we cannot know. Polanyi is taking up this position when he states, 'Though every person may believe something different to be true, there is only one truth.'[4]

Although rather confusing, this psychological analysis of truth claims does indicate why considerable conflict is liable to arise in the community, for the individual scientist is strongly committed to his truth claim and the community of scientists are strongly committed to theirs. If they disagree then the dispute is liable to continue, as there is no way either of them can reveal or be absolutely sure of the actual truth.

Two important insights into the nature of decision-making within the community can be gleaned from this analysis: the process of discovery for the individual scientist can lead to error, and the decision of the community may be in error.

The process of discovery can lead to error, although it is unlikely that the discovering scientist will perceive his error because of the very process of making a discovery, and in any case there can be no absolutely certain demonstration that he is wrong. In other words an individual is fallible even though he may be incapable of recognising his fallibility. He will have made his judgments within a particular interpretative framework and indwelled within his research. His conscience, which commits him to reveal the truth, will heighten his commitment to his theory, as he will have already, before he puts his new theory to the community, have rigorously criticised its contents, and it will have stood up to the criticism. Polanyi also argues that interpretative frameworks are often strengthened by attacks on them, and combined with this is the argument that when a commitment to a particular judgment has finally arisen then there is a tendency just to ignore conflicting evidence.

Nevertheless Polanyi does find examples of when interpretative frameworks have been weakened and finally abandoned,[5] at least in theory conflicting evidence may eventually lead to the demise of a framework. In any case, as the support of theories and interpretative frameworks is a matter of belief and not knowledge, they are open to the force of persuasion which can destroy the belief.

The decision of the community can also be wrong. This can be clearly seen within Polanyi's own argument for as an individual scientist can be wrong in spite of the fact that he has passed through the process of indwelling then no claim can be made that the aggregate of beliefs of the individual scientists is infallible.

Faith, Obligations and a Decision Procedure

The analysis of the scientific community so far brings out certain features which are common to all communities. The members of it must interact and communicate with each other, for they cannot make up a community if they are an isolated aggregate of different individuals with no interests in common. This brings out the point that they must possess shared values, and indeed Polanyi's scientists do as they believe reality exists and that it can and should be revealed. Yet although they interact and have certain values in common the members retain a degree of independence, for they have their own beliefs and ambitions, their own interests and research. Nevertheless they do and will cooperate. We can say that they have limited altruism. They can also make correct judgments and incorrect judgments, and are therefore fallible creatures. Their fallibility is increased by the fact that the information they have will never be complete. They have to make judgments while knowing in the back of their minds that their judgment may be wrong, and while knowing that the information on which they are likely to base their judgments is also open ended and incomplete. Clearly then, as in any community, we must expect disputes about what decisions should be undertaken. Disputes by their very nature tend to rip communities apart. They can sometimes be resolved by argument and sometimes they cannot. It is in fact much easier to set up a method for settling disputes than settling individual cases. A method set up and decided on beforehand can in a sense settle disputes indirectly without the direct conflict that individual combat entails. Indeed it can be argued that if a community is to exist for any length of time, it must have a method of settling disputes which its members are prepared to accept. It must have a decision procedure.[6] It is the method of spontaneous coordination by all mature scientists which is the scientific community's decision procedure.

However, as we have already argued, the scientific community can be in error and so can the individual scientist, so he may well feel justified in continuing to argue for his discovery. Yet it is the scientific community that decides whether the new discovery should be accepted as part of scientific knowledge. It is the scientific community's decision procedure that gives truth claims the status of being scientific knowledge, and gives them temporary stability so that they in their turn can be used to judge innovations.

Polanyi then has argued that it is the task of the scientist to try and understand a reality beyond our senses. As this is so then it must be impossible to provide criteria that will give certainty to this understanding, the scientific community has to rely on the emergence of a consensus in order to judge the validity of a theory. This notion of a consensus basing its decision on present knowledge is a reasonable method for judging a theory's validity, as one always attempts to check a new piece of information against information one already possesses. One tries to fit the new information into the framework of knowledge which one already has, and if it does not fit in one is naturally sceptical about its validity. Yet Polanyi does not entirely rely on the notion of consensus to maintain the credibility of the community. Three connected theories are complementary. They are a theory about the commitment of the scientist, a theory of obligations, and a theory about the unity of the community.

We have seen that within his theory of knowledge Polanyi introduces a notion of commitment to one's beliefs, and to the truth. We have examined the function of commitment within the context of individual discovery-making but we are now looking at it within its social context. Knowledge, Polanyi claims, does to a large extent arise from commitment and therefore the lay image of the impersonal, coldly detached scientist is incorrect. The scientist exhibits a heuristic passion and it is only by this emotional attachment to his research, when science becomes virtually the scientist's life, that he achieves knowledge. This emotional immersion in research and the resultant commitment to each stage of discovery means that the scientist becomes so attached to his theory that he is bound to declare truthfully what he has discovered.

This leads us to the theory of obligations. The scientist is obliged to declare truthfully what he has discovered. His conscience, and actually his task, force him to do this. Scientific morality depends on whether or not the scientist has revealed what his conscience dictates, and that his obligation to do this is threefold: to himself, to other scientists (to the community) and to reality itself, and that the first two obligations are derived from the third.

This recognition of an obligation to reality leads us to Polanyi's third complementary theory. The scientific community is a community which is bound together by faith, and the mutual task of apprehending and revealing reality. It does seem, in fact, that this model Polanyi produces of the scientific community could be applied equally well to a theological community. For instance both Polanyi's scientist and the theologian are concerned with the task of apprehending and revealing a reality beyond our senses, and like Polanyi's scientist the theologian is emotionally bound up with his work.[7] The ethics also seem very similar to the ethics of a Lutheran who is bound by his conscience, and more strictly to the ethics of William of Ockham who argued that we can never know whether or not we have perceived God's will but that we must follow that which we believe is His will. As there are no definite means of knowing whether we have arrived at the truth we must follow that which we believe to be the truth. This is really the only answer to the problem of knowledge when we move to the world beyond our senses but equally why we could say that this is not knowledge but merely unconfirmed opinion.

Of course the kind of knowledge that Ockham and Polanyi refer to is a subjective knowledge, even though we make a universal claim for it (we claim that it is objective). And being subjective or personal it certainly leaves the way open to schisms both in science and theology. Ockham in his orthodox mood, would counter the tendency by arguing that we should rely on authority or specifically on the revealed scriptures which the Universal Church had accepted — for historical reasons Ockham was bound to put great stress on authority. Polanyi makes the same move and states that personal knowledge is checked by the scientific community with their present knowledge, really interpersonal knowledge, i.e., personal knowledge which has been accepted as objective or universal knowledge, and that therefore the decision they make is justifiable, although it provides no certainty. Yet his main stress is on the originality and personal knowledge of the individual scientist because it is through him that science has to develop. We have seen that within this explanation there is room for a considerable amount of dispute between the individual and the scientific community. Generally this is controlled by the community; recognition that originality is necessary for progress, by the community being bound together by a mutual faith, and by the discovering scientist's own recognition that his colleagues also have an obligation to the truth (reality), and that the test of acceptance is the only way to continue the development of a unified science. In other words he will accept the decision but continue to hold that his theory is correct, and work within the community while trying to find additional evidence and argument to support his theory.

We have seen that the method of consensus is a reasonable method for judging a theory's validity when there are no personal criteria which can give certainty. The evidence a scientist produces in support of his theory has also to be reasonable but what is accepted as reasonable evidence also depends on the community's estimate of what is reasonable. And the consensus of opinion as to what is reasonable can change. For instance, the evidence in favour of extra-sensory perception is not considered reasonable enough. The combined weakness of theory and weakness of evidence prevent extra-sensory perception from being classed as part of scientific knowledge. In the case of psycho-analytical theory we have a powerful theory which almost succeeds in achieving a place for psycho-analysis in scientific theory. It fails because the supporting evidence is not reasonable enough. E.S.P. then is well away from being scientifically acceptable but psycho-analysis is a doctrine in a community on the borders of established science. However, it is possible that the consensus as to what is reasonable can change and a theory become acceptable because the supporting evidence becomes acceptable. The evidence, for instance, for Galileo's telescope was suspect but eventually became acceptable. It may be that this idea that the reasonableness of evidence in science depends on the consensus as to what is reasonable has to be laboured. In the case of what is reasonable evidence in law the argument that it depends on present-day opinions as to what is reasonable is more easily seen. For instance, much of the evidence accepted as reasonable evidence at witchcraft trials would be now considered unreasonable. Finger prints once considered unacceptable as evidence are now considered powerful evidence. To say then that a consensus is a reasonable method of testing a theory's validity, and that such and such evidence is reasonable depends on what we believe is reasonable and on what other people will accept as reasonable. It is a matter of judgment on our and their part.

Yet there are certain procedures which would be considered reasonable and certain criteria by which we may judge reasonableness.[8] For instance, to what extent is a theory internally consistent? Does the argument receive support from the factual evidence or does it seem to contradict it? If it contradicts it then this is a good reason for supposing that it is incorrect. Is a generalisation derived from an accepted number of instances? For instance, it would be unreasonable to say all swans are white after seeing one swan but not so unreasonable after seeing one hundred swans, and even less unreasonable to say most swans are white after seeing a hundred swans. It would be reasonable to say that I have seen only a hundred swans so I cannot really say all swans are white. But would it be reasonable to say that I have only seen eight million swans and all are white but nevertheless I cannot really say all swans are white? It would be possibly unreasonable but correct and the caution very wise. Yet a scientist who repeated the same experiment eight million times and always got the same result but nevertheless felt that he should continue doing the experiment in case one day he got a different result would not be considered unreasonable but mad. It would also be reasonable to base one's decision on one's previous experience, no matter how small it was, with a group where no one but oneself had any experience.

It would also be reasonable for the scientific community to base its decision on a new theory according to its previous experience in the field of that theory, as well as the factual evidence and the argument actually produced by the discovering scientist. The scientific community besides the individual scientist is the only group that can make a decision. But why does it have to make a decision, for cannot it just be said that unfortunately the knowledge held by the community is not adequate enough to make a judgment for no one is a complete expert in the particular field of the theory? It has to make a decision in order to decide whether a theory should be taught, whether further research should be financed, and because it is the body which scientists accept as their decision making body. The decision can take a number of forms — an acceptance, an outright rejection, or a suspension of judgment, and in this case funds would probably be made available for further reasearch.

What then can we say about the notion of reasonable evidence in experimentation, when we can make a reasonable decision that is correct, a reasonable decision that is incorrect, a reasonable decision by refusing to make a decision, be unreasonable but correct in making our unreasonable decision, and be unreasonable and incorrect in not making a decision? The analysis firmly brings out Hume's point about the weakness of the inductive method but it also indicates that the reasonableness or unreasonableness of a decision need have no necessary connection with the correctness of a decision. As I have pointed out this is why Popper attempts to develop a hypothetico-deductive method and why Polanyi relies firmly on faith. We can say then that a judgment of new theory based on the generally held beliefs of the scientific community is a reasonable method, a justifiable method, for making a judgment but even so can be in error.

This then is Polanyi's picture of the community of pure scientists. He has developed theories about the nature and understanding of reality, and as can be expected these theories have largely determined his notions about the structure of the scientific community. He in fact has produced a complete philosophy of science. He produces a theory about reality: an ontology. He explains how the scientist achieves this knowledge by what he calls the process of indwelling and tacit knowledge: an epistemology. He explains how this knowledge can be tested in spite of the fact that much of it lies beyond appearances. It is tested by the consensus of opinion within the scientific community. However, this approach necessitates an addition if it is to provide a reasonable explanation of the scientific community as it is. If it is not possible to verify or falsify a theory by some conclusive methodological test the way seems open to charlatans and to people who are just prepared to introduce theories which will be acceptable to the consensus merely in order to further their own career. Polanyi is able to protect himself against this conclusion by introducing an examination of the internal ethics of the scientific community. He provides a theory of obligation: a deontology. He also explains how science progresses by the process of individual initiative controlled by authority.

Polanyi has produced a highly interesting model of one of the most professional of all communities, the scientific community. It has certain key characteristics. It is autonomous in that it controls the development of its own ideas. It has a body of systematic ideas which it uses to control innovations. It is authoritative but necessarily allows innovations, or to put it another way it is bound by tradition but allows the controlled development of initiatives. And it is bound together by a mutual faith and mutual obligations. Polanyi wants to argue that all intellectual communities with systematic ideas are like this and that with modifications it can be applied to other communities with coherent ideas. I argue that this model is in reality a paradigm example of the functioning of a professional community.

But just how far does this model reflect the real world of

science? In the real world the scientific community exhibits an internal power structure which seems to challenge the consensus image which Polanyi formulates. However, a philosophical theory is not bound by the facts but is intended to provide an explanation of them. The question is whether the explanation is adequate, and whether it heightens our understanding of the work and structure of the community. Can the explanation maintain its integrity when it is challenged by the actual workings of the scientific community? This is important for we have previously been looking at the sort of education required to operate within these different modes of experience. Not only the Polanyian concept of the acquisition of knowledge but the Oakeshottian emphasis on learning skills and making judgments seem particularly apposite to the model.

In order to answer this question I intend to provide in the next chapter a brief and restricted analysis of the scientific community, considering points that are most likely to discredit Polanyi's system and see how the system is able to cope with the challenge.

Notes

1. M. Polanyi, *Personal Knowledge* (Routledge, London, 1958), p. 138.
2. Ibid. p. 308.
3. 'The Republic of science realises the ideal of Rousseau, of a community in which each is an equal partner in the General Will'. Cf. M. Polanyi in the new introduction to *Science, Faith and Society* (Chicago University, Chicago, 1964). The Rousseaunian General Will was, of course, infallible.
4. Polanyi, *Personal Knowledge*, p. 315.
5. He cites the case of Arthur Koestler giving up a Marxist framework, and Karen Horney giving up a Freudian framework.
6. J.R. Lucas, *Principles of Politics* (OUP, Oxford, 1966) produces these characteristics as part of the make up of a political community and indicates why a decision procedure is necessary and must also be part of that make up.
7. Cf. Paul Tillich, *Systematic Theology* (Chicago University, London, 1955), p. 26. 'He the theologian looks at his object with passion, fear, and love . . . The basic attitude of the theologian is commitment to the contents he expounds'.
8. Reason can be considered public in two senses: (a) its workings can be made accessible through the use of language; (b) as it is public it is open to tests which are applicable to the subject under consideration. For instance, utterances that did not satisfy the basic rules of language would be considered unreasonable so it would be necessary for a reasonable argument to at least satisfy such rules. An argument that met this consideration would still be unreasonable if it ignored accepted procedures for judging or testing something. For instance, an argument which indicated a person was judging the weight of some material by its size without taking into account its mass would be considered unreasonable.

6 THE SCIENTIFIC COMMUNITY: ACTUALITY AND MORALITY

The question arises at this point as to how far Polanyi's model of the scientific community actually coincides with the real community of scientists. Does it as an ideal model actually bring out its essential features or is it a utopian model merely expressing wishful thinking?

There would seem to be four main factors which are important in the internal power structure of the scientific community: the existence of a power structure; limited financial resources; the method of recognising the validity of new theories, i.e., how is it to cope with innovations; and the natural competition which exists between people with similar skills.

For the purpose of the analysis we define members of the community of pure scientists as independent scientists who have become authorities in their own area of science. We also accept Polanyi's insistence that all members have authority[1] but we disagree with the claim that they have equal authority. We argue that they have unequal authority and that the structure of the community favours the older and more established scientists[2]. Within the community we would expect the older members of the community to move out from their position of authority as their flair for original research declines, and as the chores of being involved in administration effect their position of being masters in particular areas of science. One would expect them to remain venerated but honorary members of the community. This appears to be true of the real elder statemen but it would appear that there is a period of time between their most productive period and their virtual retirement, when they are able to retain authority because of their control of the institutionalised positions of authority.

On the whole the older scientists have more authority than the younger scientists because, by the very nature of things, they are more likely to be entrenched in positions of power.[3] The fact of becoming established creates a tendency towards the older scientists being in positions of power, although the tendency is relative to members of the scientific community and not the outside community. The older scientists are more likely to hold the posts that give control of the purse strings. They often have more time to give to administration as they are no longer attempting to carve out a career. One could even say of some of the older scientists that they have more time to give to administration as their flair for successful research has declined as they have aged. Yet even if we admit that there exists an establishment in the community which will control the institutionalised posts of authority and power within the scientific community, and through them control the purse strings, can we say that in the area of knowledge there is also a tendency towards control by this establishment? I think we can. The older scientists or the establishment will tend to favour, indeed, are almost bound to favour, the beliefs and theories which they themselves hold.[4] The consensus of opinion will lie amongst the established older scientists. They are bound to defend the ideas which they believe to be true. They can defend them by four methods: by their own authority: by control of the purse strings; by control of academic appointments; by control of publications.

The control of the limited funds available for research is probably the establishment's main weapon in protecting and developing the accepted beliefs of science. It is more likely to give major grants to established scientists because these scientists have already proved their worth.[5] The established scientists are able to bring greater authority to their claims for money, and are often in a position where they can bring extra scientific pressure to bear on grants committees. For example, they may be a personal friend of a member of the committee, and then be more likely to be in a position where they can argue their case on an informal personal basis. The scientific establishment will tend to give to the younger, less established scientists, only if they believe that the area of research where they will be undertaking their work will be fruitful. Otherwise they will accept the younger scientists' theories as valid only if they fit into accepted prevailing theory. This applies equally well to the established scientist as to the not so established, but an established scientist is more likely to have a controversial theory accepted because of his greater authority and reputation and because he will be more adept at scientific politics,[6] and better placed to undertake them.

Disputes arise when the community judges whether or not a theory should be accepted as part of scientific knowledge. The controversy which rages amongst philosophers of science as to whether or not it is possible to verify or falsify a theory, or whether it is not possible to do either, is a reflection of these disputes, and even an extension of them. The original verificationist position, as put forward by A.J. Ayer, that a meaningful statement must be verifiable either analytically or empirically would really rule out the possibility of science's existence: an empirical science is not analytical like geometry and its theories cannot be verified empirically beyond all doubt. Karl Popper, in order to avoid the difficulties created by the doctrine of the verificationists but wishing to retain the possibility of testing theories, developed his own methodology of falsification. He found that a theory of verification could not provide an explanation of the progress and development of science, while his method of falsification could. In other words a theory of verification could not provide an explanation of the real world of science, and a theory of science must do this if it is to be a philosophy of science and not pure epistemology. As we have already seen, Popper's explanation of scientific methodology and scientific progress became the dominant theoretical explanation of the methodology and progress of science from an objectivist position. And certainly it is the case that his philosophy of science can provide a theoretical explanation of scientific discovery and progress for his theory, as a theory, does work, and it would be possible for science to progress in the way Popper suggests. Nevertheless there is a considerable amount of historical and sociological evidence which suggests that his doctrine of falsification is not able to provide an accurate explanation of the real world of science, i.e. it is too far from the real world of science, and at best is prescriptive in that it offers an improved methodology for science. Rather than stating that science progresses under the doctrine of falsification it suggests that it ought to progress under this doctrine. In other words if the Popperian methodology was taught to pupils as the method of science it would not be teaching them what scientists really did but what they ought to do, or a philosopher caricature of scientific activity.

Paul Feyerabend, for instance, produces some historical evidence which gives weight to the argument that science does not develop in the way Popper suggests. He argues that Copernican theory was continually being falsified, and yet continued to be accepted and eventually became the dominant theory. He argues:

> A more detailed study of historical phenomena . . . may create considerable difficulties for the view that the transition from the pre-Copernican cosmology to Galileo consisted in the replacement of a refuted theory by a more general conjecture which explains the refuting instances, makes new predictions, and is corroborated by the observations carried out to test the new predictions . . . while pre-Copernican astronomy was in trouble (was confronted by a series of refuting instances the Copernican theory was in even greater trouble as it was confronted by even more drastic refuting instances), but that being in harmony with still further inadequate theories it gained strength; and was retained, the refutations being made ineffective by *ad hoc* hypotheses and clever techniques of persuasion.[7]

Feyerabend is considering a situation where the paradigms or consensus breaks down, and its replacement is not absolutely established. The replacement theory manages to stay in the field by its agreement with other new theories which are themselves not established, and by clever use of propaganda. Individually the theories could not continue but as a package they provide a strong persuasive force.

Even within his own arguments Popper admits that in certain cases science may be too unsophisticated to allow a theory to be falsified. However, he does suggest that a theory should be presented in such a form that as our knowledge progresses we can test it by the method of falsification. In the meantime we will have to estimate its worth by the accepted opinions of the experts until a more accurate decision can be made when the hoped-for development in instrumental technology comes about. Popper in fact makes a distinction between the logic of testing and the methodology of testing. Although it is logically possible to falsify a negative existential statement by the production of one counter example, in practice a theory will not be accepted as falsified until a number of falsifying examples have taken place. And, of course, the decision as to how many falsifying examples are needed will depend on the position of the theory within the general framework of knowledge of the scientific community. Its final rejection, if that is to come about, will depend on the decision of the scientific community.

The sort of decision that is made is an internal political decision of the community and comes about after a careful weighing of the evidence, beliefs, values and prejudices. It is the type of decision Polanyi has called spontaneous co-ordination which allows the community to arrive at a consensus, and also that described by T.S. Kuhn, who arrives at his own analysis of the process of consensus, through a sociological-historical examination of the scientific community. Polanyi, of course, does not arrive at his notion of consensus because of any historical or sociological study of the community but because it is necessary for his philosophy. It is necessary to have a theory of consensus because he believes that there can be no conclusive tests which can allow one to estimate a theory's worth. Yet it is possible that a consensus will not arise or that it will collapse. This apparently causes great difficulty for Polanyi's arguments about decision making in the community, even if we consider his concept of consensus as no more than a euphemism for the result of political interplay and propaganda. Indeed it would appear that in such cases there is no way a decision can be made. The decision procedure is ineffective. (The same problem arises with Kuhn's analysis.) The danger is that, if the theory is important enough and scientists begin to take sides, the very existence of the community is threatened.

We have argued that a political structure can be found in the scientific community which creates a certain amount of age conflict between older established scientists, and the younger less established scientists. However, far from being disadvantageous to the community this age conflict allows the community to have more flexibility than might otherwise be the case. It allows the community to exist as one body. If we had a community where equal authority existed, as in Polanyi's ideal model, there would be no room for age conflict. A younger scientist would be less likely to accept an adverse decision as regards the acceptance of his discovery. The likelihood of an extreme reaction against the decision would be increased, and there would be a much greater tendency for the scientist, who had failed to agree with his colleagues, to be forced out of the community. Whereas in a situation where a tendency towards a gerontocracy existed he would know that the passing of time would be more likely to favour his theory as the younger scientists, including himself, aged. He would be likely to continue to work within the community, whereas if a near gerontocracy did not exist he may well leave. The actual community tends to tolerate indiscretions, and provides a greater degree of protection for the younger scientist than Polanyi would allow. In fact Polanyi does provide an explanation of how conflict is coped with while not directly relating it to the age structure of the community. This comes in his explanation of how the community's decision procedure operates. The community, in deciding on a theory, institutionalises the decision and attempts to make it in an impersonal way, based on seemingly objective criteria. In this way it is able to prevent to a certain extent the direct clash of committed adherents.

It is also possible that an accepted theory may not be accepted in the same way by the community as a whole. Quite possibly a theory will have different connotations in different areas of science, and furthermore an established theory may be altered by workers in the field (as has happened with Bohr's correspondence principle).[8] It would appear that in modern science, as in the days of its early formation, there need not be a consensus of opinion as to the content of an established theory. Specialisation may have weakened the authoritative structure of the community, and it may be that the interlocking network of knowledge which Polanyi described no longer exists. If this is the case then there can be no consensus, or at least a consensus will be far less likely to come about. Much more reliance has to be put on argument and influence than on the community's real knowledge of a discovering scientist's speciality. His theory could be no longer judged by generally accepted belief. It could be argued that this in fact would give much more power to the establishment. The argument being that if a theory is not certain then even greater note must be given to the opinions of the acknowledged masters of the subject. Yet I doubt if this is the case. A major factor in the power of established scientists is their position as guardians of established theory by which they judge new theory, but if it becomes difficult to provide a consensus their power is weakened, although not destroyed as they still have their own authority and experience in scientific politics.

Warren Hagstrom[9] has painted an even more startling picture of the scientific community, where professors steal ideas from other departments, where provisionally formulated ideas are too quickly expanded because of the pressure of publication from a career point of view, and where the ideas of PhD students are scooped by more experienced scientists who are able to work at a much faster rate than the students.

It would seem then that the evidence of some historians of science and sociologists seriously challenges the picture of scientific methodology formulated by philosophers of science, and certainly destroys the lay picture of the scientific community as made up of cold, calculating professionals who impersonally undertake experiments, and whose discoveries and theories have to meet the critical appraisal of fellow workers. The evidence also seems to be casting doubt on the notion that theories are tested by impersonal evidence with the suggestion that in reality they stand or fall on the political skill of their propagator.

Faith, Obligations and Commitments

It is certainly the case that the argument that the work of Sir Karl Popper on the methodology of science does not provide a true picture of the scientific community, as it does not take into account the social relationships of its members, would be a truism. But, of course, it is not intended to do this. Popper opens himself to this sort of criticism as he has a tendency to slide between description and prescription. That is, by explaining how the scientific community ought to behave he at times seems to be explaining how it does behave. What he is doing is bringing out certain features of the community which are essential for its task and formulating them into a formal methodology. He then proposes that this should be the method of science. His doctrine of criticism is really essential for the continuance of science. He effectively shows that scientific knowledge is tentative knowledge and that therefore it must be open to criticism, and that the method of criticism is not entirely destructive but can lead to the corroboration of theories, and the growth of science. It is an attempt to lift science out of the social relations of the community and a rejection of the personal authority of its members. It is stating that theories have to stand on their own feet and is, in a sense, an acceptance of the authority of the theories themselves rather than the people who put them forward. It looks at science as a system of ideas developing separately to the whims and practices of its practitioners. The doctrine of criticism prevents science from developing into a dogma, as Aristotelian science did, but of more importance at the present time it continues to provide or recommend the method of science as the method of continual criticism.

It is also the case that Polanyi does not accurately describe the power-play that exists within the scientific community but again it is not his intention to do this. His theories are in a number of respects complementary to those of Popper, after all both are realists. Popper is mainly concerned with the logic of discovery and makes use of the logical truism that a negative existential statement can be falsified by one counter example. Nevertheless, he does recognise that in practice a theory would have to be falsified a number of times before it would be recognised that it was inadequate. In other words he does recognise that some form of agreement would have to be made by the community as to the worth of a theory. This is a practical recognition that even in a highly specialised and intellectual pursuit like science the estimation of a theory's worth cannot be entirely withdrawn from the social relationships that lie within the community. Criticism, objectivity, the attempt to mathematise science remains but still there is a necessity for a decision and a decision procedure. The political or social nature of the scientific community cannot be denied but is not Popper's real concern. Polanyi, of course, puts great emphasis on this nature and on the decision procedure, and on the individual's pathway to discovery but he still recognises the objectivity of the task, and that the critical element has to be a major part in the make up of the community.

There is then much in common in the theories of Popper and Polanyi but it is Polanyi who develops the model of the political working of the community with his theory about the network of knowledge, the concept of spontaneous co-ordination and consensus. Yet we have suggested that this model covers up much of the infighting that goes on in the community, and also does not provide an adequate theory to explain what will happen if the consensus breaks down. How far then can his model of the scientific community cope with these criticisms?

His model is an ideal model of the community as it brings out certain features which he considers to be of major importance, for instance, the obligations of the members of the community, their pursuit of truth, that is their professional integrity, the nature of commitments within the community, how individual scientists interact with other scientists and the nature of scientific decisions. He is also concerned with tying in his ontology and epistemology to his analysis of the community, that is he attempts to explain the operation of the community in terms of them. His model then is limited in scope.

However, he still needs to be able to cope with some problems which can arise within the community because his model is not a utopian model but purports to bring out certain features of actuality. If, as sometimes happens, a consensus as to the worth of a theory does not arise how can his model cope with this situation? He has denied the possibility of conclusively testing theories so must chaos therefore reign? Two of Polanyi's doctrines seem relevant here: the notion that the community is bound together by faith, the community as analogous to a religious community; and the notion that the community is bound together by interlocking obligations.

The faith of the community is that reality does exist and that it is the task of the community to discover and reveal what they themselves believe to be truths about this reality. Each individual scientist has an obligation to apprehend and reveal truths about this reality: to himself as he would be otherwise denying his own task and faith, and to his colleagues who are bound with him in a common task and faith. Likewise he, as his colleagues, has the obligation to judge theories according to his own beliefs (conscience). If he did not judge theories according to his strongly held beliefs, and if he produced his hypotheses when no commitment had arisen, it would be far more difficult and perhaps impossible for the community to proceed with its task.

The difficulty of testing theories or even arriving at a consensus about them means that great reliance has to be placed on the scientist's honesty. Scientific morality comes to the forefront in the existence of the community. Polanyi's claim that the scientist is covenanted to the service of reality, and obliged to declare the truth as he sees it, becomes the paramount factor in the community's continued existence. And this far from rules out the Popperian doctrine as a doctrine of continual criticism of all theories, for by keeping up a criticism the scientist is helping to fulfil his obligation to the truth. The description of the community does not rule out the political element or power-play that exists within the community, such as the attempt to get allies, the use of propaganda, techniques of persuasion, etc., for these are expressions of the scientist's commitment to the truth, and part of his attempt to uphold and establish the hypotheses to which he is committed. The description also allows in the attempts to merely further one's career, or even the stealing of other people's theories, as without the possibility of lapses obligations cannot exist. Like all theories about ethics a theory about the ethics of the scientific community must allow the possibility of a wrong or a right action. If one is to act morally it must be possible to act immorally.

Polanyi's model of the scientific community then is able to cope with actuality. However, it does lay great stress on certain elements in the community's make up. Whereas Karl Popper looks at the scientific community from the point of view of the logic of scientific discovery Polanyi mainly looks at it from its moral aspect.

Notes

1. Cf. *Science, Faith and Society*, op. cit. new introduction. 'There are differences in rank between scientists, but these are of secondary importance: everyone's position is sovereign'.
2. For example the mean average age of the British science Research Council in 1966 was 56.27, the mean average of Cambridge Professors of Science was 57.1.
3. T.S. Kuhn has pointed out that the whole training of a scientist tends to create an acceptance of authority and a reluctance to deviate from the norm. Cf. 'The Essential Tension: Tradition and Innovation in Scientific Research' in C.W. Taylor and F. Barron (eds.), *Scientific Creativity: Its Recognition and Development* (John Wiley and Sons, New York, 1963).
4. Cf. S. Toulmin, 'The Complexity of Scientific Choice: A Stocktaking', *Minerva*, Spring, 1964, also believes that there is a tendency towards a gerontocracy in the scientific community. But see Zuckerman and Merton in M. Riler *et al.*, *Ageing and Society* 1972 who suggest that older scientists are at a disadvantage.
5. For instance, Tswett's introduction of chromotographic techniques in 1906 was only recognised in the 1920s. It was impossible for an unknown Russian botanist to get the funds necessary to establish his techniques or challenge the authority of the established chemists.
6. Thomas Huxley once stated: 'You have no notion of the intrigues that go on in this blessed world of science . . . merit alone is very little good; it must be backed by tact and knowledge of the world to do very much'. Cited in W. Hagstrom, *The Scientific Community* (Basic Books, London, 1965), p. 104.
7. P. Feyerabend, 'In Defence of Classical Physics', *Studies in History and Philosophy of Science*, vol. 1, no. 1 (May, 1980), p. 64.
8. Cf. P. Feyerabend, 'Problems of Microphysics' in R. Colodny (ed.) *Frontiers of Science and Philosophy* (Pittsburgh University, Pittsburgh, 1962).
9. Hagstrom, *The Scientific Community*.

7 EDUCATION, CONTROL AND THE JUDICIAL COMMUNITY

Polanyi argues that the analysis he has made of the scientific community can be applied to other communities which have established a body of systematic ideas. He attempts to apply a similar analysis to the judicial community in *The Logic of Liberty*[1] and to the community of historians in *The Study of Man*.[2] Both these are intellectual communities which are concerned with developing systematic ideas about the nature of justice and about the nature of the past. However, he has a further claim that his analysis can be applied to non-intellectual communities that have developed coherent ideas, for instance, the moral community and the political community, and that these coherent ideas will be used to assess and control innovations.

He uses, then, the scientific community as a prototype for the study of other communities and attempts to show that the scientific community, far from being different to other communities, has the same characteristics with its ideas progressing in the same way. Its only difference lies in its attempt to develop much stricter criteria of acceptability for innovative theories.

His analysis has contained two important elements: a belief that knowledge can only progress under the control of tradition, or, as I call it, under the control of the interpersonal knowledge which is held in a community; and an educational theory which puts great emphasis on learning by experience.

By the words 'interpersonal knowledge' and 'tradition' I am referring to the beliefs people generally accept and believe to be true. In this sense our commitment to these beliefs can be said to be a claim that the beliefs are universal, that they are knowledge. They are interpersonal because they are held within a group, and it is the group's claim that their shared beliefs are universal that leads me to call their beliefs 'interpersonal knowledge'. However, the use of the word 'tradition' is slightly complicated for we can have the tradition of a particular sub-community, e.g., the scientific community, and mean not only the scientific theories which the community possesses but its general way of looking at things such as the obligations of the scientists, its methodology and general values. We can also have the tradition of the differing sub-communities taken all together. And finally we can have the core tradition of all sub-communities, that is, the tradition they have in common. It is this third meaning of tradition, which we can refer to as the interpersonal knowledge of the community as a whole. In Polanyi's ideal community this would include transcendental obligations to reality or the truth, the operation of individual initiative under the control of authority, and the exercise of authority by reference to the interpersonal knowledge of the community. It would be by gaining experience within such a tradition that we could develop the necessary equipment for working within a free society.

In fact Polanyi uses the term 'truth' as a generic term to mean truth, justice and ideals. Possibly we can accept that in intellectual communities we have an obligation to reveal these transcendental ends, and that this could also be so in the moral sphere but it is not obviously the case in politics. For instance, Oakeshott would argue that politics is concerned with keeping the ship of state afloat rather than aiming at any particular end. However, it is a position other philosophers have upheld, notably John Stuart Mill, whose picture of his ideal community is much more akin to an academic community searching for the truth than a political community. Polanyi, nevertheless, does look at politics from an essentially moral position and is able to make his generic term 'truth' applicable to it.

Polanyi's theory of learning is based on his concept of tacit knowledge, 'We know more than we can tell.' I will briefly explain this again. For instance, it may be possible for an expert golfer to describe the swing, perhaps even to illustrate it diagramatically, to indicate how one should place one's legs, to show how one should hold one's head, and perhaps grip the shaft but this in itself will not create a good golfer. He may recognise that his explanations are not enough, i.e., he knows more than he can tell, and then demonstrate the stroke with the hope that the pupil will pick up the unspecifiable elements that cannot be explained, or rather which can be explained but the explanation cannot in itself create the expertise. This can only be achieved by imitation and practice.

Polanyi argues that a good example of this type of teaching at university level is in practical classes, where much time is spent on trying to teach students to identify cases of diseases, to recognise different specimens of roots, plants, and animals. He argues:

> But can it not be argued, once more, that the possibility of teaching these appearances by practical exercises proves we can teach our knowledge of them? The answer is that we can do so only by relying on the pupil's intelligent co-operation for catching the meaning of the demonstration. Indeed, any definition of a word denoting an external thing must ultimately rely on pointing at such a thing. This naming-cum-pointing is called 'an ostensive definition' and this philosophic expression conceals a gap to be bridged by an intelligent effort on the part of the person to whom we want to tell what the word means. Our message has left something behind that we could not tell, and its reception must rely on it that the person addressed will discover that which we have not been able to communicate.[3]

Polanyi's argument is really more than this: we learn by being shown and by imitating, but this still is not enough. We can really only learn by imitating and doing, and this applies equally well to intellectual as practical activities — but we must also become obsessed. We must, to use Polanyi's word, 'indwell' within the activity, and make it an extension of ourselves. Obviously we will not necessarily become an expert by imitation and obsession but these are necessary steps on the way to expertise, and eventual independence from our master.

The expert does not actually know the extent of his knowledge in the sense that he can lay it down for all to see. The extent of his knowledge lies within his capacity to know, to understand, and to do, and his expertise is his power to cope with problems within his own discipline.

Through our capacity to indwell we are able to build up large areas of knowledge we know explicitly but also large areas we know only tacitly. However, a real understanding of this explicit knowledge can only come about because of its existence within this framework of tacit knowledge. Polanyi, in fact, defines education as something we can only be aware of subsidiarily. 'Education is latent knowledge, of which we are aware subsidiarily in our sense of intellectual power based on this knowledge.'[4] To put it another way we cannot know the extent of our knowledge or education but we can be aware of a mastery over the subject matter in question. This leads Polanyi to state:

> We are clearly aware of the extent and special character of our knowledge, even though focally aware of hardly any of its innumerable items. Of these particulars we are aware only in terms of our mastery of the subject of which they form a part.[5]

Education then is power, and for Polanyi the term to be educated means to have the ability to control one's subject. In the intellectual sphere this will mean to have developed the conceptual powers to recognise not only instances of things we know but new instances, and fit them into our framework of knowledge. It really means we bring stability to these new items of knowledge by controlling them and fitting them into our framework. We make them understandable to ourselves.

Polanyi's concept of education then is a dynamic one. It is not a matter of first assimilating knowledge but a matter of assimilating, understanding, and having the ability to use that knowledge. However, it is not just a matter of using the knowledge in a passive way when problems arise but an attempt to look for problems and control them. It is an attempt to achieve. He argues that it is the mark of an educated mind to constantly add to its conceptual framework by assimilating new experiences and thereby constantly modifying its existing framework.

This concept of education at first sight might seem authoritative and conservative but this is only a superficial view. Polanyi is making the point that the education process can only develop from an existing framework which gives stability to our perceptions, and from this point of view it must be authoritative. We have to have confidence in our knowledge base before we go out into the unknown. The leap into the unknown is not a random leap with little chance of success but a controlled leap aimed at something we already recognise but intend to bring under our control. The idea of control within an authoritative framework is very similar to Oakeshott's development of intimations, and differs only because of the Polanyian concept of external reality. This leads Polanyi to argue that we move from the reality we know to the reality we do not know, whereas the Oakeshottian argument would be that we give ourselves a deeper understanding, a better interpretation.

A person, then, when making a decision will be immersed in the tradition of his own community, and will have built up his own concept of that tradition, as well as his own method or style of coping with problems. His decision will be derived from his own conceptual framework but at the same time it will have arisen out of the tradition or interpersonal knowledge of the community within which he works. The reason for this is clear for the individual's own framework has developed the way it has because of his own practice and experience, and education within that tradition. The decision at this stage is then offered up to other members of the community to be examined, checked, and criticised.

The aim of education is therefore to build up a knowledge of the subject matter in question, and to make the pupil adept at applying the knowledge in new situations. The knowledge will be to a large extent tacit or latent knowledge, which the pupil knows he possesses but cannot specify, and this knowledge will provide the base which will allow him to approach new problems, attempt to understand them, and find solutions to them.

Polanyi's analysis of the nature of knowledge and the learning process, as Oakeshott's had done before, pointed out that state interference was most likely to be counter productive. But the analysis had done far more than this for it had laid bare the nature of the learning process in the most professional of professional communities, the scientific community, and had attempted to show that his analysis of learning, of knowing, and of controlling knowledge was applicable to intellectual and non-intellectual communities alike so long as they presented either systematic or coherent ideas.

I now propose to examine three such communities in order to see whether this claim can be upheld: (1) the judicial community, as an example of a professional community operating not just as an intellectual community but also within the practical world of public administration; (2) the historical community operating as an intellectual community; and (3) the moral community, a non-intellectual community operating within the practical world of decision making.

The Judicial Community

In the case of the judicial community we have a profession

controlling a body of knowledge which has been built up and developed over many generations: a body of knowledge which is a common possession. Polanyi describes this graphically when referring to a judge making a decision with reference to common law.

> Consider a judge sitting in court and deciding a difficult case. While pondering his decision, he refers consciously to dozens of precedents and unconsciously to many more. Before him numberless other judges have sat and decided according to statute, precedent, equity and convenience, as he himself will have to decide now; his mind, while he analyses the various aspects of the case is in constant contact with theirs. And beyond the purely legal reference, he senses the entire contemporary trend of opinions, the social medium as a whole. Not until he has established all these bearings of his case and responded to them in the light of his own professional conscience, will his decision acquire force of conviction and will be ready to declare it.[7]

The act of a judge then is a responsible act based on his knowledge of the law and checked by his commitment to justice. The judicial decision is an interpretation of existing law which at the same time as reinforcing it modifies it in some respect. But it is more than this. Polanyi argues that the operation of common law constitutes a system of adjustments between succeeding judges and the general public. He states:

> Such coherence and fitness as this system presents at any time is the direct embodiment of the wisdom with which each consecutive judicial decision is adjusted to all those made before and to any justified change in public opinion.[8]

It would seem therefore that there is at least one similarity between science and the law and this is that both possess a systematic body of ideas which on the whole is stable but which does over the years change its contents. Yet there is an obvious difference in the activity of the judge and the scientist. A judge is given a case to decide whereas a scientist chooses his own problem for investigation. But, nevertheless, the scientist like the judge accepts a tremendous area of previously established knowledge.

He also takes account of prevalent scientific speculations, and this can be considered as analogous to a judge who refers to precedent and statute but at the same time interprets in the light of contemporary thought. Polanyi calls this process of adjustment, which seems common to the activity of a judge and the scientist, a process of consultation. Even so, although there is a similarity in the process, the method of adjustment by which the scientific community comes to a decision is not entirely analogous. His decision cannot be rejected or accepted by the consensus of his peers for it remains a judicial decision whether they agree with it or not. It is true that certain criticism can be made of the decision in the law journals and elsewhere but as such they cannot deny the decision as the scientific community can deny a discovery. The decision can, of course, be rejected by a higher court which will take into account the judge's reason for his decision, his conduct of the trial, the precedent to which reference was made and so on.

Polanyi also argues that the judicial community is a spontaneous order backed by persuasion. He states:

> This type of adjustment is exemplified by two opposing counsel trying to win over the jury to their side. When such a discussion goes on in wider circles, each participant adjusts his arguments to what has been said before and thus all divergent and mutually exclusive aspects of a case are revealed . . . The persons participating in the controversy by which the result is achieved, may be said to cooperate in a system of spontaneous order . . . in a controversy that is both sincere and fair, the participants will primarily aim at presenting the truth, relying on it to prevail over error. Therefore, I suggest that co-ordination involved in a sincere and fair controversy should be classed separately as a system of spontaneous order based on persuasion.[9]

This quotation indicates that Polanyi is attempting to make a direct analogy between the administration of justice and of science. The analogy to a certain extent is acceptable as ideally the participants in a trial should act in the way he suggests but the comparison is between the activity of one trial and that of the scientific community. It is not between the activity of the judicial community as a whole and the scientific community.

If we look at the term spontaneous order then it must mean that activity develops from within that order without promptings from the outside. To say that the scientific community operates as a spontaneous system means that it is self controlled in its activity. As Polanyi points out we can only regard it as a spontaneous system when it follows its own task of revealing reality. It can no longer be regarded as spontaneous if it follows utilitarian ends as these are prompted from outside the community. If this is the case then can the judicial community be considered as a spontaneously operating system when a judge takes into account when making a decision 'the entire contemporary trend of opinions, the social medium as a whole'? In other words the decision of a judge will be influenced not just by the case in hand and its relationship to the tradition of law and precedent, but also by an outside factor: the climate of opinion in the social world outside the judicial community.

It can be argued that a spontaneously co-ordinating judicial system would have to ignore such outside factors. Answers to legal problems could only be arrived at by working out, and then applying the logical implications of legal rules and precedents. In this case the function of the courts would be to work out, and apply along deductive lines of thought, the principles contained in the law as it stood. The courts would be isolated from policy and the climate of opinion, and the sole duty of the judges would be to apply the principles laid down in the law. It would be a far easier task to substantiate a claim of spontaneous co-ordination for this type of positivist neo-Austinian community but Polanyi seems nevertheless correct in arguing that a system of law does not operate in this way. It is fortunate that it does not, as such a system of law would only work after it had achieved a considerable degree of sophistication. The basic principles of law would have to be well established, and it would be necessary for deductions from them to be able to cope with legal problems that were likely to arise. It is probably imposssible to formulate a code of law that can cope with all circumstances and this is why we need judges with interpretative powers. Even so it remains the case that a conceptual system of law can allow for the interpretative powers of judges within a deductive framework. The problem arises when it is necessary for a new principle to be introduced and this can happen even within a highly developed system of law. The necessity for the introduction of new principles arises not because of difficulties within the already existing system of law but because of developments outside the legal system. For instance, the development of trade unions necessitated the recognition that trade unions possessed legal rights.

In fact there is necessarily a continual reference to developments in society and movements of opinion. The most obvious example is in the field of pornographic literature and its capacity to 'deprave and corrupt.'[10] At different times and places literature at one time held to deprave and corrupt can no longer be considered to do so. Public morality changes, and our estimate of people's capacity to be depraved and corrupted changes also. Indeed the insertion of such vague phrases as capacity to deprave and corrupt into legislation invites judges to take account of the moral climate of opinion.

It would appear then that the structure of certain laws makes it necessary for judges to take account of the climate of opinion before arriving at a decision. It also appears that new developments in society may necessitate the introduction of a new principle into the legal system. In this latter case the judges will attempt to fit the principle into the body of existing law, as well as taking into account the developments in society that necessitated its enactment. In the former case a judge's decision will be based on a fine balance between interpretations of the law and case precedents, as well as a consideration of the social climate. A failure to arrive at a correct balance will give grounds for a successful appeal.

Nevertheless it does seem that it is the desire of the judicial community to have a completely equitable system of law where each part is consistent with the other parts. When a new principle is introduced the attempt will be made to fit it into the prevailing system even if it does appear the judges are interpreting away the wish of the legislators.[11] In effect they are asking the legislature to think again whether or not they wish to have such legislation, which the legal profession does not like and which is opposed to the systematic ideas contained within the prevailing legal system. They are therefore asking the legislature to be more explicit in expressing its wishes, and drawing its and the public's attention to the judiciary's opposition.

The judicial community is then the guardian of a system of ideas and case history which is continuously developed by the contemplation of and the extension of the notions held within it. Yet because it is closely related to a society's decision procedure it is bound to take notice of the social climate, and is particularly vulnerable to the introduction of principles from the legislature which are contrary to the principles already contained within its own system of ideas.

This analysis of the judicial community puts us in a position to answer our earlier question: 'Is the judicial community a spontaneously co-ordinating body if it takes account of social factors, and does it need to be a closed system to spontaneously co-ordinate?' The system of ideas of the judicial community is closed in the sense that it is concerned only with justice. The introduction of ideas which are not concerned with justice will tend to make inconsistent the system of ideas and destroy judicial activity. However, the judicial community is not closed in the sense that it is isolated from contemporary happenings, as part of its function is to take note of contemporary happenings in the world outside the judicial community and apply their system of ideas to them. Laws introduced merely for the sake of political expediency are analogous to the interference with science for utilitarian reasons. In other words they are an attempt to turn the judge away from his task in a way similar to the scientist being turned away from his search for truth by utilitarian interference. The task of the judge is to interpret laws in accordance with the concept of justice inherent in the law as it has developed. In this case to force a judge to apply a law that is not in accordance with the existing system of law, i.e., to administrate a law which contains a principle which is inconsistent with the principles contained in the existing system of law, is destructive of his task. As long as the legal 'machine is controlled by the principles of justice laid down by the law and interpreted by the legal profession',[12] it remains an independent spontaneously co-ordinating intellectual activity, and is analogous to the scientific community.

Yet is it possible to bring the analogy between the two communities even closer? For instance, is the scientist's search for the truth analogous to the judge's search for justice? It is part of Polanyi's argument that the scientist's search for truth is a search for a truth about an external reality, and that the system of ideas that make up science contains the scientist's beliefs about the true contents of reality. Truth about external reality, as far as it is available, is contained within the system of ideas of science. In the case of justice the truth about justice is contained within the system of law, interpretations and case history which make up the law. But can we consider reality and justice separate to man which man only interprets and expresses in his two systems of ideas? The scientist is trying to say something about a reality that exists in fact, and judges are trying to reveal and apply a principle which exists as an abstraction. For the scientist reality exists independently of himself, that is, it would still exist even if he was not there, although his interpretation of it would not. For the judge justice would not exist if he, or more correctly the human race, did not exist as it is an abstraction of the human mind. However, this will not make a difference to the operating of the two systems of ideas. The reason for this is that spontaneous co-ordination operates because of the existence of interpersonal knowledge within each community. The truth about reality, for practical purposes, lies within the system of ideas of science, and the truth about justice lies within the system of ideas of the law. This is why innovations either in science or law are judged by the truth, as far as it is known, which is held within the system of ideas of the two disciplines, and why innovations have to be consistent with these ideas to be accepted.

A further similarity between the two communities lies in the scientist's and the judge's indwelling in their subject and their commitment to the ideas and values of their disciplines.

However, there does seem to be a difference in the relationships of scientists with each other as compared with judges. Science contains a competitive element, a striving for individual advantage that is not so immediately apparent in the judicial community. A judge cannot advance his career by new initiatives in law but rather by demonstrating the certainty of the law, its unchanging structure and stability. Science, although based on the past looks towards the future, and openly does so. Innovations are therefore stressed and applauded. The innovatory capacity of a scientist is also an important factor on the career structure of science. The good scientist achieves his prominence through his discoveries and his success in meeting criticisms. The judge does not achieve success through innovations in law but ideally through perceiving and classifying what the law states in each particular case. As this is so, with the scientist a competitive element is introduced in the process of discovery; with the judge it is confined to the clear expression of existing law. The judge is a reluctant legislator whereas the scientist is an enthusiastic innovator.

In making our analysis of the judicial community we have artificially created a similarity with the scientific community by considering that the judicial community's membership is confined to the judges, when in practice lawyers also form part of the community. There is no such division of powers in the scientific community. However, lawyers are really ancillary to the work of judges. They clarify the arguments for the judge, and their function is to help him arrive at a just decision. For this reason the inclusion of lawyers in the judicial community cannot fundamentally alter the analysis.

In spite of the differences we have considered, if we idealise the judicial community, and isolate it from other areas of the community's decision procedure it is certainly possible to apply the sort of analysis Polanyi makes of the scientific community to the judicial community.

Notes

1. M. Polanyi, *The Logic of Liberty* (Routledge and Kegan Paul, London, 1951).
2. M. Polanyi, *The Study of Man* (Routledge and Kegan Paul, London, 1959).
3. M. Polanyi, *The Tacit Dimension* (Routledge and Kegan Paul, London, 1966), pp. 5-6.
4. M. Polanyi, *Personal Knowledge* (Routledge and Kegan Paul, London, 1959), p. 103.
5. Ibid.
6. Cf. a series of pamphlets for the Society for Freedom in Science.
7. Polanyi, Logic of Liberty, p. 162.
8. Ibid.
9. Ibid. p. 165.
10. Section 1 of The Obscene Publications Act (1959) provides that an article is obscene if its effect is, 'if taken as a whole, such as tends to deprave and corrupt persons who are likely, having regard to all relevant circumstances, to read, see or hear the matter contained or embodied in it'.
11. A case supporting this argument was that of Lady Duff Cooper when the Lords set aside a lower court decision under the Drugs Act (1959) that she was guilty of an offence of possessing drugs even though she did not know the drugs were on her tenants' property. The lower court decision opposed the principle of *mens rea*, and could not possibly be an interpretation which Parliament intended (sic). Also Sweet v Parsley (1970) Appeal Cases 132.
12. Polanyi, *Logic of Liberty*, p. 41.

8 AN INTELLECTUAL AND A NON-INTELLECTUAL COMMUNITY: HISTORY AND MORALITY

Polanyi sees the process of understanding as a continuous process from the study of inanimate matter to the study of history, which needs greater connoisseurship and greater identification with the subject matter of the study, as it moves through the natural sciences into the humanities. The final development of the process is man eventually turning attention to himself by the study of history and thought. He attempts to show that, as in all intellectual communities, a fruitful study of history necessitates the immersion or indwelling of the historian in the subject matter of his research. And that like the scientist the historian will approach the subject matter of his research with a certain interpretative framework, and will then judge it in accordance with this framework. The historian and the scientist in making their judgments will also rely on the standards and values of their own respective communities.

However, there is a difference, for whereas we can probably talk about the scientific community we cannot talk in the same way about the historical community. We have to talk about communities of historians or rather schools of historians. Even so it does seem possible to argue that within these different schools certain skills have been produced which have proved effective in gaining historical knowledge, and that a body of knowledge has been developed which can be used to judge innovations. To put it another way, innovations will have to fit into the existing interpersonal knowledge of the school.

Under this argument truth for a member of a historical school would consist in correct interpretations of historical phenomena in accordance with his own interpretative framework. This would be the personal knowledge of the historian, and a claim that his understanding of the phenomena was universally applicable. The claim would be accepted if it fitted into the knowledge already possessed by the school, that is, their interpersonal knowledge.

The claim would then become true as far as the school was concerned.

From this analysis we are led to argue that each school will have its own interpretative framework to which the interpretative framework of each member will approximate. The original interpretative framework of the school will have arisen because different historians with similar interpretative frameworks will have come together and decided to accept each other's mutual authority in determining the truth. The group would really be setting up a decision procedure, and they would have to do this before we could call it a school. Indeed to the extent we can show that a school is not governed by the mutual authority of its members then to that extent we can deny the existence of the school. New adherents to the school would have to fit into the style of the school. In other words their own interpretative frameworks would have to approximate to the pre-existing ideal derived from the original adherents.

It could be argued that science, on the other hand, seems to consist of an interlocking series of interpretative frameworks. The question therefore arises as to why there is not a corresponding breakdown into schools of science as there is in history and, for instance, theology. There seem to be three reasons for this.

(1) The subject matter of research necessitates a more personal involvement, so whereas in science more often than not an argument will be confined to criticisms of methodology, really a criticism of the scientist's competence, to attempts to indicate the failure of a theory to fit in with other theories, and mere career competitiveness, another factor will enter in the case of history. This would be an attempt to challenge the historian's interpretative framework (a challenge that would rarely happen in science), for instance, a challenge from a Marxist point of view.

(2) Scientist's do not develop mutually exclusive schools based on different moral interpretative frameworks, so, although there are schools of thought in the sense that there is a disagreement over specific points, this does not effect the whole outlook on science. It is the moral factor in the interpretation of history that creates the schools. It would be extremely difficult for a Marxist historian to accept a Whig interpretation of history as the truth: all he could do would be to accept it as a Whig interpretation of history.

(3) The methodology of science tends to hold it together, for instance, the use of experimentation, statistical techniques, rules for presentation of findings. In fact there seems to be a general consensus as to the technical approach to the subject matter of research but this is not the case with history.

Generally then, with the qualifications given it does seem possible to apply some of the concepts in Polanyi's analysis of the scientific community to the different schools of history. The analysis produces a rather formal and ideal version of the actual situation but nevertheless it does seem a reasonable interpretation not too far from reality.

The Moral Community

As we have seen, the analysis Polanyi has made of the scientific community can be applied to other communities concerned with intellectual pursuits and also an intellectual community which has to work in the practical world, the judicial community. We now wish to show that the analysis can be applied to a non-intellectual and a non-professional community: the moral community.
Polanyi sees morality as made up of two different elements: a moral passion and energy which is immanent in all men, and a striving towards the transcendental. He states, 'The mentally healthy person is the person who lives by love, reason and faith, who respects life, his own and that of his fellow men.'[1] This mentally healthy person then allows his moral fervour to be led by transcendental values, and internalises these values by his apprenticeship in a community. Morality has an internal and external aspect. However, this twofold division in the nature of morality makes it possible for moral passion to be split from its goal, the striving towards the transcendental. Polanyi calls this a pathological situation, and a case of moral inversion,[2] where the moral passion can be attached to some non-moral or immoral goal. We can therefore have homeless moral passions operating within a materialistic framework or a moral passion becoming attached to some evil end.
A person struggling with a moral problem dwells in that problem and looks outwards towards independent principles. Indeed if no principles applied to the situation there could be no

moral problem. Yet for Polanyi morality is not just recognised in the formal application of principles, for it is the skilful application of these principles which is important. Morality is expressed in action and not by mere reference to formal principles and rules, and indeed no morality can be explicitly set out in its entirety. There is therefore an uncertainty in the scope of the principles and rules to which we refer and in their correct application.

This analysis of moral problem solving also reveals something about a moral personality. A moral person should not be annoyed and harsh in his judgment of others for he will know that a moral activity is an arduous activity based on deliberation and skilful judgment but also tinged with doubt. He will therefore be compassionate, loving and sympathetic — a case of epistemology blunting the edge of moral passion.

The moral person operates in a moral community and they will watch his actions and examine the principles he refers to, and the precedents he follows. The process can be formally analysed.

His actions will be judged on the following criteria: (a) Is the action a moral one, that is, is the person obeying a moral rule which he claims has universal validity, and that therefore it should be applied in all circumstances that have the same relevant characteristics; (b) If the rule is acceptable then is the action consistent with the rule he claims he is following; (c) Is it applicable, that is, is it the right rule to apply in the circumstances; (d) Is it justifiable in terms of the moral code of the community? If these criteria are met then we can say the action will be accepted as a moral action.

However, let us consider the case where some of the criteria are not met. For instance, if the act is not consistent with a rule then it could be that the moral claim is fraudulent or perhaps mistaken, and if merely mistaken then the actor could perhaps be persuaded he was in error. It could be that the rule was not applicable in that it was either irrelevant to the circumstances or was ranked incorrectly with others or perhaps that it was given an improper weighting when compared with some other rule that pointed in another direction. Again, with advice this could be corrected. The action could not, of course, be immoral as when we consider applicability the assumption is already made that the rule to some degree is acceptable to the community. The requirement of justifiability would require that the rule was acceptable to the community, or put in another way, that it was or would be accepted as part of the moral knowledge of the community, that it was the right one to apply in the circumstances, and that the action was consistent with the rule.

Again the open textured nature of moral judgment, the recognition of the difficulty of solving problems, etc., will mitigate the punishment for the unskilful, the weakminded, and those who have not the courage to set out on the moral task.

It is possible then to analyse the moral community in the way the scientific community has been analysed. It may appear, however, that this type of analysis is destructive of the distinction between normative and scientific laws. In fact it is not, but what it does do is point out that there are close resemblances between the gaining of knowledge in the material or scientific sphere and the gaining of knowledge in the moral sphere. Both forms of knowledge are gained by attempting to understand our experiences. Moral understanding is an attempt from a special point of view to understand personal and social experience by developing interpretations about them. It formulates norms of conduct, which if accepted by a group of people as a basis for criticising and praising their own and other people's actions — as binding on them — becomes part of the moral values of the community. We could say that they are given the value of factual existence within that community. This does not mean that they exist as tangible facts but that they do exist as generally acceptable rules of conduct within that community. In the case of science the scientist formulates an interpretation about facts. The interpretation is then put to the scientific community as a theory, and, if it is accepted, it becomes part of the scientific knowledge of the community. Likewise this does not mean the theory is a tangible fact but it does mean that for the time being it exists as a statement about the real world which claims to be a correct interpretation of that world.

In fact, of course, we cannot write of the moral community as such for there are many moral communities but nevertheless the same analysis can apply. A claim that a moral rule is a moral rule will have to be accepted by more than one person if it is to achieve the status of moral knowledge. It must be judged by at least the claimant's own community. As in the scientific community a claim to universal knowledge can only be accepted if it is recognised by other people. Moral knowledge like scientific knowledge cannot be purely subjective knowledge, but has to be public knowledge or rather interpersonal knowledge. It can only become public knowledge when it is accepted by other people as having a universal character.

When we make a claim that our moral rule or action is right we are also claiming it is right for others. However if this claim is not accepted by others despite our supporting reasons then the action cannot be said to be morally justifiable. It cannot be justified because either we have failed to relate our action correctly to an acceptable rule of morality, or the rule is not acceptable as a rule to others. In other words its claim to universal validity is not acceptable to others. Of course in such a situation we may not give up our claim, for our moral passion and commitment will make it unlikely that we will give it up lightly, and it is more likely that we will try and persuade others that we are correct. Nevertheless as long as our arguments are not accepted it cannot be said we are acting morally in undertaking the action or following the rule but only that we are claiming to act morally.

Under this analysis we have conceived of moral knowledge as existing within a community, that is, a body of beliefs acceptable to a community. An actor will be bound by the traditional values of his own community, that is, he will be obligated to follow the values and rules of that community, and to a certain extent he will have internalised through the process of education the moral norms of that community. The actor's moral code will therefore be similar to other members of his community but will not be exactly the same, as he may well have interpreted norms in a slighly different way, he may have accepted norms from other communities and therefore internalised conflicting norms, he may have made his own additions. In such a case, although the code will be similar to others it will be his own, and as he matures and moves out of his apprenticeship, he will be responsible for it and to it. It will be his own personal morality or rather his claim that its contents can be called morality.

As I have already pointed out there is a difficulty in such an analysis as there are a number of moral communities with possibly different codes of morality. Under the argument we have used we have to argue that a moral rule is a moral rule if it is accepted by a particular moral community. To achieve the status of being a moral rule it must be accepted by someone other than the claimant. A moral rule or norm comes into existence when a group of people accept it as binding on them. We can say they have created a decision procedure which decides which norms they should follow. Such a procedure can exist with only two people so at the extreme we will argue that a moral rule can exist if it is accepted by more than one person. We can claim universal validity for it but it does not have to be universally accepted as a moral rule but nevertheless it has to be accepted by someone other than the claimant.

We have in the moral community all the characteristics that Polanyi considered in his analysis of the scientific community; the individual actor who has been initiated into the practices of the community but who has become responsible for his own actions; the members of the community acting as the guardians of traditional knowledge and spontaneously judging innovations in accordance with that knowledge; the heuristic passion; the acceptance by each member of the status of the decision procedure; the commitment of each member to a transcendental idea — the truth. His concept of moral passion is of great importance for it is apparent that it is this moral passion which is at the basis of commitment and the heuristic task. Really for Polanyi the search for the truth is the highest form of morality. The commitment of the scientist to his discovery, his truth claim, can be explained by this moral passion. Hence Polanyi's objection to the attempt to turn pure science to utilitarian ends for it diverts it from its moral crusade. Truth is used as a synonym for other transcendental values such as justice and fairness, and it is because all the communities considered have this commitment to transcendental values that they are able to operate. They have some other concern than an internal power struggle.

In developing his theory about the nature of the scientific community he puts great stress on the element of personal knowledge, where the individual scientist through a deep deliberation in his work finally arrives at a judgment he believes to be true, and then puts it to the scientific community for acceptance into the body of scientific knowledge. Yet we also have the interpersonal knowledge of the community where its members judge innovations by their network of knowledge. The judgment again is only made after a deep deliberation by the people who are the guardians of the traditions of that community. But this picture of the scientific community is also a reflection of the moral community making a moral decision.

Polanyi originally used the scientific community as a prototype for the study of other communities, and in developing his analysis he came to recognise that the only way such a community could work was by a commitment to a transcendental ideal, the truth. And by interlocking obligations to the truth, and to their own nature as moral men, and to their colleagues in their intellectual community who were the guardians of their knowledge. Both the authoritative nature of the community and the freedom of the individual scientist to honestly innovate were both essential elements if science was not to degenerate into either a dogma or fantasy where individual innovation became all encompassing. As Polanyi developed his studies it became apparent that the scientific community could not be used as a prototype to study other communities for it really reflected in a more obvious way characteristics that existed in other intellectual communities. And these characteristics were in some way a reflection of characteristics that existed in the moral sphere; deep deliberation, passion and commitment.

It is the concept of commitment which becomes so important to Polanyi, and a commitment to the truth. Commitment to a non-transcendental end, a material end, meant disaster. This obsession with the truth even led Polanyi to develop a theory of evolution where there is, in all men, a vital force which strives always to achieve the truth. Even the political task had to be in a wide sense nothing else but an unconscious attempt to strive towards the transcendental.

Yet is not a lot of what Polanyi says correct? How can intellectual communities operate unless they strive to achieve the truth? There is really no other reason for their existence. Oakeshott puts it in another way. They are striving to achieve coherence, a completely stable and coherent view of the world. But for them this coherence is the truth.

Intellectual communities then strive to achieve the truth, and one indication that the truth has been achieved is that the systematic ideas which are being developed exhibit a coherence. It is also the case that we can consider these intellectual communities as paradigm examples of professional communities. Can it be argued then that all professional communities must have the features which have been apparent in this analysis?

Professional Communities

What are these features that have become apparent? The first thing to note is that the communities have developed a language which is appropriate to the discipline. Yet the language does not exist by itself. It is not a meaningless jargon but is designed to express in a more precise way the ideas which are essential to the discipline. Jargon to the outsider may be confusing and create a barrier to understanding but it is not intended to do this. It is intended to act as an appropriate tool in the expression of the nuances and distinctions of the discipline to the members of that discipline. This brings out another feature, for the specialised language is a tool to express and develop the systematic ideas of a discipline. Systematic ideas are also essential to a discipline. We cannot talk of a discipline unless we are able to recognise that it has in its possession a body of systematic ideas. Likewise I would argue that a profession to be classed as a profession must have developed its own appropriate language and possess its own body of systematic ideas.

Why, it may be asked, must they be systematic ideas, why not any old ideas? The answer is clear for unless the ideas are related to the task they are irrelevant, and there is no need to develop any specialised language or systematised ideas. When we are concerned with a particular task we begin to sort out ideas which are relevant to that task and irrelevant to it. When we have sorted out the relevant ideas we try to fit them together in a way that is appropriate to the task in hand. We begin to systematise them but we go further than this for inconsistencies are worrying and suggest we may be mistaken. We therefore try and iron out inconsistencies and achieve coherence.

Yet who is to decide on whether coherence has been achieved or not? A discipline and a profession only comes into existence when a decision procedure has been set up. The decision procedure's function is in effect to guard the systematic ideas of the discipline from subversive ideas, and to decide when new ideas can become part of the knowledge of the discipline, i.e., it gives new ideas the status of knowledge or the truth, and also decides when old ideas must be thrown out.

This brings out another feature a professional community must have, for it must be autonomous. This means that not only must it be a separate discipline with its own language and body of knowledge but that it must control its own discipline. The members of that discipline through their decision procedure must control themselves and decide what is relevant to the discipline and what is not. Outside interference is not only liable to be uninformed but challenges the independent nature and autonomy of a discipline, and suggests that it is something other than it is. For instance, the attempt to plan science for utilitarian purposes suggested that applicability was the task of science and not the furtherance of knowledge.

A proper profession must at some stage have developed its own process of education. It has to be prepared to show its pupils the language, and the application of the discipline, and inculcate the ability to become equal partners in the practice. To become in effect independent mature members of the profession with the possibility of innovating within the framework of the profession. The community's authoritative function will include not only this educational function but its function as the guardian of the systematic ideas of the profession.

However, the authoritative function extends even further than this for as guardians of the ideas of the profession it has to have the authority and power to take action against members who transgress the moral norms of the profession. The decision procedure of a community must be able to inflict sanctions on the fraudulent and immoral. It has to defend the moral integrity of its profession as otherwise the profession will collapse. Some writers on professional ethics, who refer to professions that not only possess a body of ideas but are client oriented, tend to develop a theory of reciprocal ethics between the client and the professional. This indicates that it is to each other's mutual benefit to treat each other fairly. However, as can be seen by my argument, not only will immorality in terms of the discipline bring the profession into disrepute but it will threaten the very solidarity of the profession. When there are no impersonal tests which can guarantee the stability of the profession's knowledge then it can only rely on the integrity of its members, i.e., that they are not acting fraudulently or out of self interest.

Clearly this analysis of a profession has to take account of the fact that many professions are not as innovative as the scientific community. For example the judicial community is bound to be more conservative, as would an individual church in dealing with theological innovation. I am suggesting, however, that a profession cannot properly be called a profession unless it possesses the features I have discussed.

Notes

1. M. Polanyi, *Knowing and Being* (Routledge and Kegan Paul, London, 1969), p. 245.
2. Polanyi, *The Logic of Liberty* (Routledge and Kegan Paul, London, 1951), p. 106.

9 ARGUMENT AND PERSUASION

Both the works of Oakeshott and Polanyi suggest that the education of a professional person must be far wider than it first seems. A pupil must become not only skilled in the language of his discipline/profession but become a master practitioner who is skilled in the art of rhetoric and persuasion but nevertheless is bound by the moral obligations of his community. In this chapter I will examine the role of argument and persuasion, and see what it entails within a professional community.

One of the interesting features of both Oakeshott's and Polanyi's writings is their approach to the concept of tradition. It is not a body of information which is handed down from generation to generation, a body of rule-like propositions which each new generation must learn and then attempt to apply. It is far more a way of going about things which is not expressed and to a degree is not expressible.

Oakeshott, in reflecting on the nature of political decision making, points out that when we make a decision we will bring with us a whole bunch of different beliefs, prejudices and feelings, as well as moral and prudential maxims which may be applicable or not. We will also have certain skills in estimating the consequences of actions as well as beliefs about the world around us. In so far as these beliefs can be considered normative they will not be self consistent but may well point in different directions, and cannot therefore be satisfied at the same time. This means that they cannot be used as a body of norms or principles which can automatically point to us the right course of action. These beliefs, prejudices, feelings, etc., Oakeshott calls a tradition and he says that his use of the word is actually intended to indicate that they are not a self consistent set of principles, and that although relatively stable they can change. We learn this tradition from experience and it does not appear before us in the form of propositions but perhaps in the form of practices and institutions.

The question arises as to how, if the tradition does not lead to decisions, it informs us. He points out that it is practical discourse which is the process by which we find out from the tradition what we should do, and how we should go about justifying our proposed actions. We find out from our tradition 'intimations' which are aids to reflection rather than pointers in a certain direction, 'What is sought is a decision which promises the most acceptable balance in the circumstances between competing goods.'[1]

On the other hand, for Oakeshott, the attempt of science is to lift itself out of this traditional and uncertain world and an attempt to become 'a world of absolutely stable and communicable experience.'[2] What in fact hinders the full development of science are practical interests for they prevent science moving into the abstract. He argues, 'Scientific observation is designed expressly to replace observation in terms of personal feelings by observations of an absolute stability, by quantitative measurement.'[3] Science then, as for Polanyi, consists in systematic consistent ideas aimed at coherence. Yet as science aims at coherence or the truth it cannot make compromises. In political and practical discourse we can and do argue in favour of compromise; in science we cannot. This is important for the operation of the scientific community because disputes will clearly arise and arguments will take place. I will argue that although the ultimate aim of scientific activity is to establish systematic, consistent and stable ideas the pathway to this creation is not all that different from practical and political discourse.

The paradigm form of rational argument is the deductive form as in geometry. In geometry we start from a given premise and progress to a conclusion which is consistent with that premise. We can decide beforehand what is relevant and what is not; for example, in discussing the nature of an equilateral triangle we can consider questions as to the colour of the triangle irrelevant, and the questioner stupid. The form of our progress is 'so and so therefore so and so therefore so and so'. The key word is 'therefore', and an argument is either consistent with the previous argument or it is not, and if it is not it can be ruled out. This brings out another feature of a geometrical argument for it is either sound or it is not. Weak arguments are no arguments at all. This ideal model of rational argument is the grail to which philosophers of science have always been striving. Thomas Hobbes in his scientific approach to the study of society adopted the model of the geometrician in *The Leviathan*. Descartes in his *Discourse on Method* also took geometry as his model, and the attempt to mathematise all science has been part of the attempt to force science into a deductive framework.

Political and practical arguments are different. We cannot set out beforehand what is relevant and irrelevant for relevance will depend on the circumstances of the case. Often weak arguments are better than no arguments at all. A political argument like most practical arguments is dialectic in form. The argument goes 'so and so therefore so and so' and then someone else comes in 'but so and so therefore so and so'. The key word is 'but'. There is a logic of one side of an argument and a logic of the other side of an argument.

We have seen that science cannot be entirely deductive for a purely deductive argument lies in the field of geometry, mathematics and logic. The natural world is not tied together by the rules of logic. One object is not tied to another by logical necessity. This was the point David Hume made, and for him this meant that science was not possible as we could not move from particular events that we observed to generalisations about other events. This led Popper to accuse Hume of allowing his argument to degenerate into a philosophy of belief, and why Popper himself developed his hypothetico-deductive model of scientific progression. However, as we have also seen, Popper has not been able to lift science entirely out of the real world where we have conflicting opinions, beliefs, prejudices, and preferences into the realms of logic. Polanyi's own analysis of discovery and its assessment stresses this point even more. Scientific argument cannot be purely deductive but like political argument has to be dialectic in form. This is often not recognised as published papers are presented in a deductive form, and they do approximate to the paradigm of rationality. They argue a case but nevertheless another case is frequently available. Of course compromise is not possible in science — whereas it is in politics — because scientists are committed to the truth. But what this means in practice is that much more skilful rhetoric and persuasion is needed than in politics to overcome an opponent's objections. Arguments still have to be produced in a rational and impersonal form even when a theory is under heavy attack. Personal abuse is not allowed even though it is not unknown.

The need for persuasive skills are needed because of the nature of knowledge. We cannot know for certain and our estimates of knowledge are based on our own judgments. We have seen that

Polanyi has argued that it is only through faith and commitment to our beliefs, and with the control of a community with a like-minded commitment, that we can move closer to an understanding of reality. It is the mutual obligation to the truth which guards against the excesses of persuasion but it is also this very obligation which inevitably leads to the necessity for a scientist to practise the persuasive arts. If knowledge can progress only through the beliefs of a like-minded community, then that community has to be persuaded by the innovator that the beliefs he expresses are the right ones. The discovering scientist then has a two-fold task: he must present his arguments in as objective a form as possible and he must at the same time persuade others of their reasonableness, while recognising that in fact they are a matter of judgment on his part. Let us examine again what would be an objective form.

In science, at least, the more theoretical a theory the more likely it is to be objective as it is a remove from contact with the commonsense world of possible illusion and prejudice. Polanyi illustrates this when discussing the relative objectivity of the Ptolemaic and Copernican cosmological positions:

> It becomes legitimate to regard the Copernican system as more objective than the Ptolemaic only if we accept this very shift in the nature of intellectual satisfaction as the criterion of greater objectivity. This would imply that of two forms of knowledge, we should consider as more objective that which relies to a greater measure on theory rather than on a more limited sensory experience.

According to this argument a theory becomes more objective as it becomes more abstract, as it breaks away from everyday perceptions. Ideally it will have an explicitness as a system of rules so that it can be clearly understood by people within the public world of science. It will be devoid of our own personal desires and idiosyncrasies for its truth is not a matter of personal taste on our part but is something which lies in the theory itself and demands to be recognised by rational creatures. The theory must stand on its own feet, be impersonal and independent of its propagator. It must have a general communicability in the way the Ptolemaic theory did not have, for we should be able to understand it whatever our location or situation. As Polanyi points out a theory has to be very like a map with its own independent status and rationality. If we fail to find our destination when correctly following a map we will consider that the map is wrong, not that we are mistaken. It is the case that we may at first think we are mistaken but when we have carefully checked through we will know that we are not wrong but that the map is — the map must stand on its own feet.

Yet this objectivity is elusive. How can we move to the utopia of objective knowledge when our knowledge of the truth is uncertain, our beliefs shaky, and our state of mind one of ignorance? How can we then move from this state of ignorance to a state of knowledge, to a state of certainty? The answer is that we can never do so but we can move to a position where we can make judgments which we can rely on to build further edifices. The truth claims we put forward have to be put forward in a form everyone can understand and check if they are going to be publicly recognised. The truth claims are personal commitments and judgments but their form in the public world of science has to be objective otherwise there can be no public assessment of their truth. This fact has to be recognised by the budding scientist. He has to learn to withdraw his commitments from the format of the theory and design it in such a way that it can be publicly debated. This does not mean he is not committed to his theory but that his commitment has nothing to do with its truth, or its assessment in the public debate. Nevertheless the fact that he is committed to the truth of his theory means that he will participate in the debate, and attempt to formulate more objective arguments (arguments in an objective format) when his theory comes under criticism.

We have seen that the scientist will approach his problem from a particular interpretative framework and that that framework will be similar to his colleagues'. It is this fact, of course, which allows his colleagues to check his theory. The mutual authority of the mature scientists working together forms the decision procedure of the community, and it is that decision procedure which determines whether or not a theory will be given the status of truth within the community. To be a professional scientist the individual scientist has to recognise that the decision procedure can make these decisions. He has to recognise that it has the authority to make these decisions but that the nature of obtaining knowledge and the uncertainty of the real truth gives him leeway. The decision procedure receives its authority as the guardian of established scientific theory — that is knowledge which has been given the status of truth — but the individual scientist is also dedicated to revealing and expressing the truth. The individual scientist then may be wrong in his estimation of the truth but the scientific community can also be wrong. The individual scientist then, although recognising the right of the community to make a decision on the status of a theory, is justified in continuing to uphold and argue for his rejected theory. He will set out by argument, persuasion and evidence to change their minds. We have seen that Polanyi's term 'spontaneous co-ordination' must be considered a euphemism to describe the disputes, debates and arguments that ensue as the community decides whether to accept, reject or put aside for another time new theories. (The Oakeshottian position would be slightly different. As there is no external reality for Oakeshott the scientist would be arguing over the relevant coherence of different positions. But this is just a different way of looking at what is actually happening.)

It can be argued that the 'truth' for an individual member of the scientific community consists of a correct interpretation of the data in accordance with his own interpretative framework. In Polanyi's terminology this would be the personal knowledge of the scientist but it would be put in an objective format and would be making a universal claim. If this claim were to be accepted by the scientific community as the 'truth' it would have to fit in with the knowledge they already possessed — it should not disturb its coherence. There is the possibility of competing claims but only the scientific community has the authority to give a claim the status of 'scientific knowledge' or 'scientific truth'.

It is appropriate here to examine the meaning of the words 'truth' and 'knowledge'. They are really ascriptive terms and defeasible. In other words they are like a badge we stick on to a theory which can be withdrawn if it can be shown that the theory does not really meet the criteria we use when presenting the badge, or if it can be shown that the criteria were the wrong ones to use.

This point is of importance for it indicates that the use of words like 'truth' and 'knowledge' are not absolute terms. This means that a scientific truth does not necessarily remain a scientific truth for ever, and a piece of scientific knowledge does not remain a piece of scientific knowledge for ever but that its status is open to argument and persuasion. Even the criteria used in estimating whether a theory is to be given the status of truth or knowledge are themselves optional alternatives and are derived from the traditional values of the scientific community, and are established by arguments which refer to those values. For example, a criterion sometimes used is beauty but how important is it and what does it mean? I am not suggesting that this is a formal process but that nevertheless it is what happens.

The hold your interpretative framework has on your approach is even stronger if we consider other aspects of Polanyi's arguments such as the concept of the master/apprentice relationship, for on entering the scientific community you are shown round it by your master (teacher), you copy him, you learn the skills, the techniques, the language and almost your way of thinking from him. You are led through the successes the framework has brought about and you are led to see the potentialities of the approach. You are really indoctrinated into it, and it is only through this process that you may one day become an independent and original scientist who has gained his own contact with reality. You learn then by doing and working in your teacher's approach.

As I have pointed out the study of the scientific community is used as a prototype for the study of other intellectual communities and eventually of society as a whole. It has been shown that even in the paradigm example of truth searching, absolute certainty is not available. We have to rely on our own beliefs and commitments but if our approach to the truth is to have any degree of certainty, and is not to degenerate into confusion and anarchy then we must work within the social framework. It must be a communal task controlled by a communal authority. Yet this analysis has also shown that as this itself cannot provide absolute certainty, room must always be available for dissent and argument. It is to the nature and form of that argument that I now turn.

Interpretative Frameworks and Rhetoric

The type of manoeuvres available to combatants in an intellectual dispute lie in three areas: a debate within similar interpretative frameworks; a clash between interpretative frameworks; a sceptical denial of an interpretative framework's heuristic potential.

An attempt at the justification of one's judgment within an interpretative framework would need to show that:

(a) The data was relevant. For instance, in looking at the annexation of property from a moral point of view the fact that the property was taken without the owner's consent would be a relevant factor, whereas the fact that it was taken skilfully would be irrelevant. The point of view determines what data is relevant or not relevant, and it also gives meaning to otherwise uninteresting facts. Likewise from a scientific point of view some facts would be relevant and others not relevant.

(b) One would need to show that the hypotheses developed within one's interpretative framework provided a reasonable interpretation of the data. That it gave an explanation that adequately or more adequately explained the relationship between the phenomena. In other words that it was applicable to and gave an increased understanding of the phenomena.

(c) That the hypotheses were consistent with other hypotheses within the interpretative framework, that is, that they did not contradict them.

(d) That any additional hypotheses used in arriving at or defending one's judgment were consistent with each other, with the interpretative framework, and with the judgment.

(e) That any later *ad hoc* additions developed in defence of one's original judgment or in development of it were likewise consistent with it. The attempt is to develop a generally coherent position.

The appropriate interpretative framework to use is often itself a matter of judgment so, for instance, it would be incoherent to use a framework based on measurement to understand the nature of God, and incoherent to use such a framework to understand the nature of goodness — thus the problem created for Benthamite utilitarianism which uses the measurement of pleasure and pain as the criterion of goodness. The point of view should actually tell you which interpretative framework is correct, although it is not as straightforward as this. And which point of view to use is also a matter of judgment, although often dictated by the circumstances. For instance, if you witnessed a murder to talk immediately about the skilful and artistic nature of the act would be eccentric to say the least. Likewise to talk about the creation of life when discussing biology, or Genesis when looking at evolution would be the wrong point of view and inappropriate for the circumstances. Much confusion arises when an inappropriate point of view is used, for instance, when a technical point of view is used when a moral point of view is appropriate, or when a religious point of view is used when a scientific one is appropriate. As I have stated the attempt is always to achieve coherence and consistency, and that is why Oakeshott, for example, argues that the truth is the same as coherence.

A counter argument within a particular argument would not challenge the point of view or the interpretative framework but would challenge the consistency of other arguments within the framework. Thus one would attempt to show that one's opponent was inconsistent within his own argument, or alternatively that the general argument was inconsistent with the interpretative framework both tacitly accepted.

Notice I have already argued an intellectual community, for example, the community of scientists will have similar interpretative frameworks but the fact that they are similar and not the same means that unresolvable disputes can arise even within the same community. Of course the disputants may think they are using the same framework but they need not be because of the very process of learning — we do not emphasise the same thing — and the unspecifiable components of the interpretative framework.

Polanyi, in fact, points out that 'coherence as the criterion of truth is only a criterion of stability. It may equally stabilise an erroneous or a true view of the universe. The attribution of truth to any particular stable alternative is a fiduciary act which cannot be analysed in non-commital terms'.[4] He is arguing that, although a batch of theories may be coherent, and to that extent rational, it is not enough to indicate that they are true. It could be argued then that 'I can see that your theory is coherent and fits in with your other theories and your interpretative framework, but I still deny its truth.' Polanyi is making the point that to claim a particular interpretative framework reveals the truth means that you must be committed to it but that a non-committed person can to a degree accept its rationality but deny its truth.

Another way of arguing this is to say that we may attempt to make our theories as objective as possible, we give them an objective format, but the nature of theories and their relationship to our interpretative framework means that the apparent explicitness of the theories hides their open-endedness. They are furry edged or leave open the way to further development or rejection. In other words they are not completely coherent in themselves and because of that may not carry within themselves the power to convince a non-believer.

The question arises then as to whether or not it can be shown that a correct interpretative framework has been used. Can we use rational arguments to support the use of one interpretative framework rather than another one? In fact if we cannot support the interpretative framework we use on rational grounds by showing that we made a free rational choice between possible alternatives, then we will be unable to establish the objectivity of the whole process. In a conflict between people who are committed to different frameworks from the same point of view the attempt must be to show that the framework one is using is more rational than the opposing one. It has greater coherence and gives a better explanation of the facts than the one with which it is in conflict. Furthermore one needs to show that it has greater heuristic potential than its rival: that it has led to a whole range of new discoveries, and that it still has the power to do so.

In a conflict between frameworks each opponent would have to be prepared to show the doubter round his framework, and in doing so he would have to make it as explicit as possible in order to reveal its dynamic potential, to show its heuristic power, and to emphasise its coherence. He would have to indicate the weakness of the opposing framework by claiming it gave inadequate explanations and was not progressive in that it failed to lead to new discoveries or predict novel events and, indeed, had to resort to the defensive tactic of inventing *ad hoc* additions to its dogma, in order to preserve itself from extinction.

The difficulties of doing this are obvious for not only has a strong rational argument to be produced but the argument must be persuasive enough to overcome the commitment of one's opponent to his own framework. In a sense one is asking the opponent to step out into the unknown with a new apparatus of which he is completely unsure.

In choosing a framework one must undertake an act of faith for after all one cannot know its potential until one has indwelled within it and become committed to it and to its revelations. The sceptic can, of course, deny the veridical qualities of any framework. Yet if he does this he cannot be a scientist, a Marxist, or a theologian for all have their interpretative frameworks with the original tentative act of faith. He can, of course, be a philosopher.

This analysis suggests that the education of the scientist, and indeed the education of anyone within a professional body which is concerned with revealing the truth, or rather making truth claims — one could almost say professional integrity — has to be far wider than is usually thought. The scientist, for instance, not only has to learn the basic skills, language and interpretative framework of the scientific community but he must learn how to put his theories into an objective format, while at the same time remaining strongly committed to them, and he must learn how to participate in controversy by rational argument and rhetorical persuasion. The persuasion is necessary because as he is arguing within a mode of experience his arguments cannot be completely coherent with all the ends tied up.

Notes

1. M. Oakeshott, 'Rationalism in Politics: A Reply to Professor Raphael', *Political Studies*, vol. 13, 1965.
2. M. Oakeshott, *Experience and Its Modes* (CUP, Cambridge, 1933), p. 170.
3. Ibid., p. 176.

10 CONCLUSION: OBJECTIVITY AND EDUCATION

Both the Polanyian analysis of knowledge and the Oakeshottian analysis of modes of experience suggest an uncertainty at the heart of the educational task, and lead us to wonder whether the ideas and traditions we pass on to our children are mere transient products. And that indeed the skills and techniques we inculcate are likewise transient products, adjuncts of those beliefs which with time vanish into a forgotten past. Must we consider all our knowledge subjective or perhaps intersubjective: the arbitrary beliefs of our own profession or discipline?

Michael Oakeshott is an idealist philosopher and has therefore been attacked on the grounds that there can be no objectivity without the acceptance of an external reality. I will look at Oakeshott's own defence of his position. However Michael Polanyi believes in an independent reality and yet has still been attacked by eminent philosophers as a subjectivist.[1]

The argument is important for if we can attach the label subjectivist to a particular writer we are really stating that his beliefs merely represent his own personal preferences (prejudices), are not supported by any rational arguments, and therefore can be ignored. Or to put the argument in a wider context we are stating that a subjectivist theory about the nature of knowledge must itself be incoherent, as it is stating all knowledge is merely subjective belief and that therefore this particular theory about the nature of knowledge must be merely subjective belief. We therefore have no reason to accept it.

I will look first at the objectivity of the theories put forward by Polanyi. The basis for the argument that he is a subjectivist lies in three areas of his thought: his concept of indwelling, his notion of commitment, and his rejection of the argument that theories can be conclusively tested.

We have seen that his concept of indwelling is based on the notion that discovery or new insights can be made only by a person who is prepared to emotionally immerse himself in the subject matter of his research. He must become obsessed with it and make it an extension of his own life. The insights he then produces are not an accident or an idea thrown off the top of his head but are based on this deep immersion in the research. This leads to a strong commitment to the insights he produces. They are something that his extensive knowledge of the subject matter has led him to believe. He believes that they are the truth and is prepared to put them forward as the truth to his colleagues, and vigorously support the universal claim he makes for them. Polanyi sees this development of insights as a progressive achievement which the researcher makes as he struggles from one insight to another. The process of indwelling then reveals, in a sense, different levels of understanding, for as one gains an understanding at one level one is then able to use the new understanding to work towards a further understanding. We have also seen that this theory of gaining knowledge is allied to a theory about a hierarchical reality, so through the process of indwelling we therefore progress from one level of reality to the next. Yet at each stage of understanding we reach we have to rely on our judgment about the nature of that reality. We have to become committed to our beliefs before we dare progress towards the next stage. It can be said that we build up an edifice of commitments, where each stage relies on what has gone before, and that the edifice comes about because of our immersion — indwelling — in our research.

This analysis of how we develop an increased understanding about the nature of things does not at first sight seem objectionable. Certainly, for instance, a number of theologians would produce a similar picture of our approach to God: the necessity for a deep faith in and a love for God before an understanding can be obtained. Indeed it is almost the orthodox approach to theological understanding. It is also analogous to the approach of the mystics but likewise even a more rationalistic approach will include within it the notion of passion, love, and faith, for instance, St Augustine's *credo ut intelligam* — I believe so that I can understand. Yet the shock treatment Polanyi produces is not to develop such concepts but to apply them to our understanding of science. The scientist is not the coldly analytic, impersonal automaton, which many writers have produced as the archetypal scientist but a person who is led by heuristic passion, is obsessed with his work, and relies on his own judgments. The shock treatment is also enhanced by the fact that, as Polanyi was using science as the paradigm example of the learning and understanding process, the analysis applied to the acquisition of knowledge in all fields.

However, if all we have are our own judgments based on passion-soaked commitments then surely any preposterous notion could be justified? A fanatical Nazi presumably also may have his own judgments and passionate commitments, and so may a lunatic. The objection is really a simple one. The fact that we are committed to something cannot be taken as an indication that it is the truth. The truth is independent of our beliefs. However, Polanyi's point is that all we have are these judgments, and, although it is the case that commitment cannot guarantee the truth, we nevertheless must expect commitment to be associated with truth claims. Indeed if the researcher had no commitment to his theory then it would be quite likely that his theory would be irrelevant.

It is the claim that all our knowledge is based on personal judgment that is hard to accept. Surely we can have more certainty than that? It is our desire for certainty that makes arguments like Polanyi's so frightening. Cannot we after all test theories and is not science, unlike theology, a body of theory that has successfully met numerous tests? This suggests that a scientific theory must be put in a form which allows us to test it, and that science as such is a body of knowledge which has been tested.

Polanyi's argument suggests otherwise. The very process of discovery works against it, for how can you know whether a theory is right or wrong unless you yourself have gone along the same pathway, and have used the same interpretative framework? Likewise his concept of the hierarchical structure of reality which progressively moves away from the tangible, and makes it impossible for us to conclusively test sophisticated theories against the physics and chemistry of matter. Yet his argument is not against tests as such but against the notion that there can be conclusive tests: that there can be some test outside the process of discovery which can come in and state whether a theory is right or wrong. For instance the Popperian concept of the logical truism that one counter instance to a negative existential statement can falsify that statement. Of course it can, it is a logical truism, but as Popper points out himself, in the real world of science we would wonder whether we had set the experiment up properly, that we had not made a mistake, and we would continue to falsify the theory until we had satisfied ourselves that it was really false. We would then put the arguments and the experiments before the scientific community, and they would examine them or perhaps repeat them, and make a judgment on our competence. Only then would they make a decision on the worth of the theory. The judgment would not be arrived at automatically by some impersonal test, but only by scientists deliberating after immersing themselves in the theories and techniques of science. Indeed for Polanyi it is part of the obligation of the scientist to do all he can to test his theory, and it is only after he has gone through the process of checking and rigorously criticising his own theory does he develop his strong commitment to it, and put it before the scientific community for acceptance.

Polanyi then does not argue commitment guarantees the truth or that we should not undertake tests, but that we should expect commitment should be associated with truth claims, and that there are no conclusive tests independent of ourselves. Clearly if we found a theory continually failed we would give it up but it would be our decision after due deliberation. Nevertheless his rejection of the neo-Kantian view of science as the study of appearance and its replacement by a hierarchical view of reality, and his psychology of discovery, associating truth claims with commitment does provide ammunition for objectors. In fact Polanyi directly argues that he is not a subjectivist but that he is trying to move away from the notion of objectivity associated with the concept of the cool detached scientist towards his own concept of personal knowledge. Indeed he opens his major work *Personal Knowledge* with an explanation of what he means by objectivity, and part of the claim is that we, in fact, attribute greater objectivity to theoretical knowledge than knowledge gained through sense experience. This was the point he was making when he discussed the relative merits of the Copernican and Ptolemaic cosmological systems. Of course, for Polanyi the reason for this was that it was revealing a higher level of reality, it gave deeper meaning to the data, and could therefore be considered more objective (more real and less superficial). The more general argument is that the greater the objectivity shown the more abstract the theory becomes, and the further it moves away from everyday appearance. This is also the basis of Oakeshott's argument about the nature of science. He then sets out a completely orthodox view of objectivity. The theory will be considered objective in so far as it has explicitness as a system of rules so that it can be understood within the scientific community. That it will not mention our own commitments as they have nothing to do with the truth. Its truth will depend on its validity not on our support for it. In other words it must stand on its own feet, be free from prejudices and be impersonal. Finally it must have a general communicability so that it can be understood from every situation or location. Notice what Polanyi is doing, he is stating that in arriving at a discovery we have to have an obsession and personal commitment but when the discovery is made we then put it before the community in as objective a way as possible so they can estimate its truth. An assessment cannot be readily made if a theory is overladen with prejudices.

The assessment of a theory, which has been put in an objective form, is then made by the scientific community or if it is a piece of historical knowledge by the appropriate school of history, etc. At this point a major question arises. We can perhaps accept the notion that a theory is put to the community in as objective a form as possible but can the community in question make an objective decision? And what is the justification for the decision making capacity of say the scientific community?

In examining the claim of personal knowledge to be classed as knowledge we come up against a fundamental difficulty. Personal knowledge comes about after the process of indwelling, and is a belief for which we claim universal validity. Yet can this really be called knowledge? In a case where a claim to personal knowledge is rejected by the scientific community, to claim that we still have knowledge, in spite of its rejection by the acknowledged authorities, is hard to justify. Yet Polanyi's whole theory of indwelling and commitment indicates that we must continue with our claim. It is possible to argue that if in fact the claim we put forward is a correct interpretation of reality, and the community rejected it, nevertheless it would remain the truth. This is so but it must be remembered that we can never be absolutely certain that what we believe is a correct statement about reality. In practice it is the theory's acceptance by the community which is used as the criterion of truth, and as our knowledge is not certain can it not be argued that this is a more reasonable criterion than the decision of one man? It would surely be arbitrary to give an individual the power to decide what is knowledge?

Apparently this must be the major justification for the

community's assessment of a theory, i.e., the decision of the individual is arbitrary but theirs is not. Yet cannot the justification also be challenged on the grounds that not only is the decision of an individual arbitrary but so is the decision of the community? The argument could be developed by pointing out that a theory could at one time be accepted as knowledge but at another time rejected. This would apply not only to theories but to methodology, language, and the methods of science. The whole body of science changes over a period of time as the badges of acceptability are either stuck on theories or withdrawn. This means that science is unstable with theories that are at present accepted always liable to be rejected at any moment of time. It therefore means that the judgment of a theory's validity by reference to the accepted ideas of the scientific community must itself be an arbitrary practice. It cannot be non-arbitrary when a decision is based on an unstable, fluctuating body of ideas.

This argument, if accepted, is devastating for it means that there can be no basis for knowledge claims, and that all such claims must be arbitrary. However, I will try to argue that it is not the case that the decision of the community is arbitrary, and I will do so on four grounds:

(1) There is no other more reasonable method of deciding on the validity of a theory. There are only two possible alternatives for judging a theory: either the individual judges his own theory and declares that it is scientific knowledge, or the theory is judged by the authorities on the subject, and they will judge it by reference to the system of ideas which have already been accepted by the community. The first alternative would be so arbitrary that we can consider it a non-starter, and even if we agreed that the second alternative was arbitrary, it would be far less arbitrary than leaving the decision to the individual scientist.

(2) It does seem to be the case that no single theory in the system of science is certain of maintaining its position within the system. But this does not mean that every item of knowledge within the system is likely to lose its place. There is a fairly stable body of knowledge that remains stable, and although it is the case that certain items of knowledge may lose their place the majority of them will not. For instance, it is unlikely that a securely established theory will lose its place, and it will only lose its place after a series of failures, and not by one dramatic refutation. Even

then it is likely to remain for restricted use. A theory gradually slides out of the system of science and it is not suddenly hurled out.

(3) The decision of the community is not really arbitrary as it is part of a task which has continued over the centuries with a good deal of continuity in method. There is also continuity in theory. New theories are developed from the old sometimes by drawing out intimations which already exist within the system of ideas. A theory is rarely blatantly false but only inadequate, and the discovery of an inadequacy often leads the way to new discoveries in attempts to resolve the inadequacy. In other words we can say that the system is on the whole stable, and is not subject to constant change in all its aspects, because every item of knowledge does not change at the same time.[2]

(4) The process of judging a theory by communal knowledge cannot be considered arbitrary as it is quite rational to judge a claim to knowledge by knowledge we already possess, and indeed we cannot do anything else.

These four arguments to justify the non-arbitrary nature of a decision of the scientific community do seem to succeed in their task. However, they have failed to indicate that whereas the decision of the scientific community is non-arbitrary the decision of the individual is arbitrary. This in fact cannot be shown for, as it is quite rational for the scientific community to judge a theory by knowledge they already possess, so it is rational for an individual to do the same. An individual, in judging the truth of his own theory will compare it with knowledge he already possesses as a member of the scientific community. And a large part of this knowledge will in any case be acceptable to that community. However, we are dealing with a claim to universifiability, and it is the recognition of human fallibility in dealing with such a claim that is a major reason for the formation of the scientific community. It is a belief that a claim is more likely to be universifiable or the truth if other people accept it. This is so although acceptance cannot give us certainty in its truth. However, it may be able to provide us with a greater feeling of confidence in its truth. The argument gets very near to the statement that majority agreement is a criterion of truth but this is not the case. What it does say is that in practice general agreement is used as a criterion to decide whether or not a theory should be given the status of truth.

We have failed then to prove the non-arbitrary nature of the decision of the scientific community as compared with the arbitrary nature of an individual decision. Both can be considered rational decisions, although the balance of the argument seems to favour a communal decision as we are dealing with a fallible human being's universal claim. We have arrived at the point where it must be admitted that as we cannot have a direct revelation of the truth the claim of both personal and interpersonal knowledge to achieve the truth has a certain degree of justification, as both can provide reasonable claims. Yet it can still be argued that in the case of science the decision of the scientific community is far more reasonable. Such an argument refers back to the structure and nature of the community. If we have originally agreed that scientific knowledge can only develop within the scientific community controlled by the joint authority of its members, and has become a member of that community then it is irrational — a contradiction — to argue that an individual member can decide on the truth of a discovery. He cannot decide himself that his theory should be taken into the body of science.

This does not mean a scientist has to give up his claim to knowledge if it is rejected by the community. A favourable decision by the community is necessary for a theory to be counted as part of knowledge, for it to be given the status of knowledge for the time being, but it is not a sufficient indication of knowledge. We have seen that the knowledge of the community is tentative and may change, and as this is the case an adverse decision may be reversed, so therefore a scientist is justified in pressing his own claim to knowledge by producing more evidence and persuading others of his truth claims.

As other intellectual communities possess a system of ideas, judge claims of knowledge by reference to their system, and admit the claim of their community to accredit knowledge, then the same arguments can be used with reference to them.

There are then a number of arguments which suggest that Polanyi's analysis of the acquisition of knowledge and its development within a community does not mean that we do not have a basis for our claims to knowledge. Even when we recognise that in accepting an interpretative framework we must at first accept it on trust, as we cannot know its veridical qualities until we have dwelled within it, we still need not accept that the process leads to subjectivity. A new apprentice can still be said to have good reasons for his choice, as he can argue that other people, whom he respects for their experience and good will, vouch for its effectiveness, and that their arguments about the veridical qualities of the framework are persuasive. It is also the case that at the beginning of the process a schoolboy who opts for a discipline or a scientist who turns towards a new discipline have some possibility of choice and therefore the opportunity to make a rational decision.

Polanyi has followed Aristotle in arguing that we can gain no more certainty than the subject matter will allow but has then argued that there is not a subject matter which will provide absolute certainty. That all knowledge must be based on human judgments and commitments and can always be mistaken. If this is the case then we must certainly change our concepts of rationality and objectivity to something more realistic based on the actuality of man's situation rather than considering that man can act like some impersonal God-like creature sitting outside actuality. But we must also recognise that if knowledge is to grow with any degree of certainty it must exist within a social context and grow within a social framework. Polanyi's epistemology inevitably leads him on from his theory of personal knowledge to a theory about knowledge in its social context, and thence to a theory of education.

Oakeshott, although an idealist, looks at the development of knowledge in a very similar way to Polanyi. Although Polanyi has a theory about external reality we still cannot check our ideas with any certainty against it. As Oakeshott argues, we have to rely on our own judgment and use coherence as a criterion of truth. Polanyi, of course, as a realist makes the point that coherence can only give us stability and cannot guarantee the truth but nevertheless, it is all we have got. In a way he hankers after certainty while intellectually realising it is impossible. Oakeshott simply argues that the sort of certainty given by an independent reality is not possible, and that the idea is irrelevant and incoherent. He also argues that the traditional notion of objectivity as some impersonal method of making judgments is also incoherent and therefore wrong. Interestingly Oakeshott does not move to a study of knowledge in its social context in the way Polanyi does. He develops his notion of the modes of experience as restricted attempts to achieve coherence, and studies the process of teaching and learning before and within these modes.

Education in a Social Setting

The combined theory of Polanyi and Oakeshott gives a complete picture of how we acquire knowledge, how we develop necessary skills and abilities, how we can be taught them, and how we can use them within intellectual and professional communities.

We acquire knowledge by using an interpretative framework as a tool to approach a chaotic agglomeration of facts and ideas. We sort them out by fitting them into the framework and by making them explicable in terms of it. In other words we stabilise them by trying to make them coherent. We therefore not only have to develop an interpretative framework but also the ability to use it. In fact all proper knowledge includes the element of 'knowing that' and 'knowing how'. This also indicates why Polanyi writes of education as a power, for education not only gives us a tool to approach chaotic phenomena and understand them but gives us the power to control them. It gives us confidence in our ability to overpower them.

Importantly when an interpretative framework has been developed, and it is used from a particular point of view, it is used to tell us what is relevant and what is not. It allows us to sift evidence and arguments, and to take into account only that which is necessary for the argument in question.

Both writers have pointed out that thought is a matter of making judgments, of deciding what is relevant and what is not, on whether something can be relied on or whether it cannot, on when to act and when to do nothing. This capacity to make judgments, and on the whole to make correct judgments, is a matter of practice. It is a skill attached to knowledge. From one point of view we can consider the whole process of education as developing the capacity to make judgments within different interpetative frameworks. This capacity to make judgments is not something we can acquire entirely by ourselves but learn from example. Thus Polanyi's emphasis on the master/apprentice relationship, and Oakeshott's emphasis on learning a style. He argues that if you cannot recognise or understand the style of a person you will be unable to understand him comprehensively.

This is an additional point to the argument that you can only understand a person if you work within a similar interpretative framework, that is, play the same ball game, but an argument that an individual's approach within that framework — his emphasis on different nuances of it, and his skill — will be personalised. It is therefore necessary if a complete understanding is to be achieved to know a person's style. Allied to this argument is the suggestion that a pupil cannot become independent of his master until he has developed his own style. He learns by copying but at some point must become original.

Professional education or education within a particular discipline is of the same type as general education but it puts special emphasis on learning the language, ideas and skills of its particular discipline. These skills are wide and include the rhetorical skills of argument and persuasion as a necessary element in the make up of a successful professional.

The different communities have the difficult task of recognising that each member must have the freedom to innovate even though he must not deviate too far from the traditional values and ideas held within a community. Likewise professional education has to be authoritative, and gradually lead an apprentice to a degree of independence and freedom.

Education, because of the very nature of the learning process, our acquisition of knowledge, and our development of it, must be conservative. It must also put great stress on intellectual honesty. If we have only our own judgments and commitments to rely on, and there are no independent tests to determine whether they are correct or incorrect, then a community cannot operate unless its members are honest. Morality lies at the heart of these communities for ultimately they are bound together by mutually binding obligations which have been developed to protect their systematic ideas from charlatans and cranks. A commitment to the truth has to be an important element in the make up of these communities. A major task then of all educational institutions must be to inculcate intellectual honesty amongst its pupils. This is not just a nice requirement or a forlorn hope, but a necessity if a cultural heritage is to continue and develop, or a professional community is to retain its integrity. And without integrity there can be no community and no profession.

Notes

1. Cf. K. Popper, 'Replies to my Critics', in P.A. Schilpp (Ed.) *The Philosophy of Karl Popper* (The Open Court Publishing Co., Illinois, 1974). A. Musgrave, *Impersonal Knowledge: A Criticism of Subjectivism in Epistemology*, PhD thesis London University, (1969). And H. Skolimowski, 'Karl Popper and the Objectivity of Scientific Knowledge' in *The Philosophy of Karl Popper*.

2. A similar justification of communal knowledge is made in W.H. Walsh, 'Knowledge in its social setting', *Mind*, vol. LXXX, 1971.

INDEX

abilities 54-6, 59
  see also skills
apprenticeship 36, 58-63, 128-31
argument 23, 24, 110-20
  rational 23, 24, 11, 119
  practical 110-12
  see also disputes
Aristotle 36, 129
authority 66, 75-82 *passim*, 100, 114, 126, 131
autonomy 67, 75, 107, 108
Ayer, A.J. 10, 22n1, 79

beauty 65, 116
belief 16, 17, 20
  see also commitment, faith
Bohr, N. 82
Brennan, J. 25, 36n3

certainty 13-15, 18, 28, 71
  Cartesian method 13-15
  Humean attack on 14, 15
  necessity 15
  problem of induction 15
  see also truth
closed system 20, 96
  see also paradigm
coherence 29-32, 35-7, 66, 87, 118, 129
  see also truth
commitment 40, 48, 67-7i *passim*, 83-6, 104-6, 114, 121-4
  see also indwelling
communicability 5, 12, 33, 125
community 65-93, 99-130 *passim*
  historians 87, 91, 99-101
  intellectuals 87, 88, 99-109
    see also community of historians, judicial, scientists
  judicial 87-99, 108
  moral 87, 91, 101-6
  non-intellectuals 87, 91, 99-109
    see also moral
  scientists 65-86, 91-3, 98-108 *passim*, 111-30 *passim*
conceptual framework 91
connoisseurship 56, 62, 99
conscience 67, 69, 71

consensus 65-8, 71-4 *passim*, 78-85 *passim*
control 87-95 *passim*, 130
criteria of acceptability 87

decision making 69, 70, 74, 81, 110-12, 126-7
  see also consensus, spontaneous co-ordination
decision procedure 69-71, 95-8, 107-8, 114-15
development of personality 54
discovery 40-9 *passim*, 69-71, 112-13, 121, 127
  see also indwelling
disputes 23-5
  see also argument, consensus, decision making
doing 55

educated mind
education 9-11, 20-1, 34-6, 51-63, 87-98 *passim* 104, 110-32
  aim 10, 54, 91
  as power 89, 90
  authoritative nature 35, 52-4, 96; *see also* apprenticeship
  imparting judgment 36, 57-62
  instructing information 36, 57, 60
  moral education 9, 104; *see also* intellectual honesty
  non-objective nature 20
  professional 110
  scientific 41, 65, 110
  types of education 52-3
experience 23-36 *passim*, 61
experimentation 74, 101
expertise 89

faith 66, 72, 83-6 *passim*, 113, 119, 122
falsification 17, 18, 65, 75, 79, 80
Feyerabend, P. 20, 22n14, 79, 80
freedom 51, 52

gerontocracy 81, 82
Gestalt (gestalten) 40-9 *passim*
  see also indwelling

133

Hagstrom, W. 82, 83
Harre, Rom 50n10
heuristic passion 71, 105
historian 99, 100
Hobbes, T. 111
Hume, D. 14-17, 22n7, 112

ideal model 81, 84
idealist 31, 46, 121
imparting, 36, 57-62
independence 52, 70
indoctrination 10, 11, 21, 51, 116
indwell 39-50 *passim*, 67, 68, 99, 121-8 *passim*
information 53, 57, 60
initiation 53, 57, 60
integrity 11, 84, 108, 119, 131
intellect communities *see* community
intellectual honesty 131
internal consistency 65, 73
interpersonal knowledge 87-91 *passim*
interpretation 24, 25, 47
interpretative framework 23, 31-5, 99, 100, 114-20, 123, 128-31

jargon 107
judge 92-9
judgment 25-8, 32-7, 40, 54-62, 67-70, 117, 118, 123
    from different points of view 25, 26, 33
    with an interpretative framework 32-4
    see also imparting
judicial community 87-98, 108
judicial decision 92-3
justification, 102-4, 111, 125-6
    moral 102-4

Kant, I. 44-7 *passim*, 124
know how 49, 130
know that 49, 130
knowledge 9-22, 30-50 *passim*, 53-6, 65-76, 87-91, 113-32 *passim*
    interpersonal 87-91 *passim*, 99, 104-5
    moral 102-5
    objective 11-13, 17-21 *passim*, 38, 40, 121-32
    personal 48, 72, 99, 125
    scientific 10-21, 30-3, 37-50 *passim*, 99-108 *passim*, 113-14, 121-9
    social context 65-75
    tacit 37-50, 56, 88, 89; focal (distal) 43-5; from-to structure 43-5; subsidiary (proximal) 43-5; tacit dimension 44; tacit integration 40-7, 49, 50
Kuhn, T.S. 18-21, 22n12, 42, 81

Langford, T.A. 45, 5n11
language 51, 53, 62, 119
law 92-97 *passim*
lawyers 98
learning 41, 49, 51-63, 87, 91, 129-30
legal profession 95
Lenin, V.I. 34

Marx, K. 33, 34, 36n17, 119
master/apprenticeship relationship *see* apprenticeship
Mill, J.S. 88
modes of experience 23, 26-31 *passim*, 51, 53
    autonomy 30
    Science as a mode 30, 31
    see also points of view
morality 9, 10, 71, 84-7, 91, 99-108 *passim*
    education 9, 104
    emotivist theory of ethics 9
    judgment 101-4
    justification 102-4
    moral community 87, 91, 101-6
    moral passion 101, 104
    moral person 102
    professional 108
    rules 102-4
    scientific 71, 84-6

Newton, I. 39, 45
non-intellectual community *see* community
normative law 103

Oakeshott 23, 26-37 *passim*, 51-63, 88, 90, 91, 110-11, 121, 129-30
objectivity 11-13, 17-21 *passim*, 38, 40, 121-32
obligation 84-8 *passim*, 106, 110, 113, 131
    see also morality
obsession 39, 49
    see also indwelling
open endedness 38, 39, 119

paradigm 18-20, 80, 81
    see Kuhn, T.S.
passion 71, 105, 122-3

perception 40-6 *passim*
  see also indwelling, tacit knowledge
personal knowledge 48, 72, 99, 125
  see also tacit knowledge
persuasion 20, 65, 69, 86, 110-20, 129
Peters, R.S. 35, 36, 58-63
philosophical theory 76
points of view 23-33 *passim*, 117-18
  see also interpretative framework, modes of experience
Polanyi, M. 3, 22n3, 23, 31-50 *passim*, 63-106 *passim*, 110-32 *passim*
political community 87, 88
polycentric system 67
Popper, K.R. 12, 16-19, 22n2, 22n6, 22n11, 79-86 *passim*, 123-6 *passim*
Price, H.H. 16, 17, 22n9
principles 56, 102, 110
professional community 106-8, 131
professional integrity 84, 108, 131
progress 79, 113

rationality 111, 118-19
realist 31, 46
reality 29, 30, 37-49 *passim*, 85, 88, 94-7, 122-5, 129
  hierarchical structure 37-9, 43
  see also indwelling, personal knowledge, tacit knowledge
reasonableness 73-5, 76n8
relativity 9, 10, 18-21 *passim*
rhetoric 20, 116-20
rules and rule like propositions 55-60 *passim*, 102-4, 110, 125

schools of history *see* community
science 10-21, 30-4, 37-49 *passim*, 65-89, 92-101 *passim*, 105-6, 110-30 *passim*
  decision procedure 69-71, 114-15
  power structure 78-86
  scientific community *see* community
  scientific law 103
  scientific method 17, 18, 65, 75, 79, 80
  see also Feyerabend, Kuhn, Popper
scientists 66, 83, 97, 99, 114, 119
  see also community of scientists
self taught 61
skills 36, 52-9 *passim*, 99, 131
  see also abilities, judgment
spontaneous co-ordination 66, 67, 81, 84, 93-7 *passim*
Stevenson, C.L. 10, 22n1
style 62, 63, 130, 131
subjectivity 9, 10, 18-21 *passim*, 121-3, 129
systematic relevance 65
system of ideas 23, 29-32, 92, 95, 96, 107, 127-8

tacit knowledge *see* knowledge
teaching 41, 42, 49-63, 88, 89, 129-31
testing 12, 17-20, 21, 80, 85
  see also falsification, objectivity
Torrance, T.S. 50n4
tradition 51, 67, 75, 87-91 *passim*, 100, 104-6
trial 92, 93
Trotsky, L. 9
truth 45, 67-72 *passim*, 84-8, 96, 100, 105-6, 113-9 *passim*, 122-9 *passim*
  as an ascriptive term 115-16
  see also coherence
two world theory 47

universifiability 72, 127
  see also objectivity, personal knowledge
utilitarian 105, 108
utopian model 85

validity 71, 73, 78, 105, 126
verification 65, 75
visions 46, 67

Winch, P. 20, 22n16
Wittgenstein, L. 20, 21, 22n5